Privacy Risk
Complete Self-Assessment Guide

The guidance in this Self-Assessment is based on Privacy Risk best practices and standards in business process architecture, design and quality management. The guidance is also based on the professional judgment of the individual collaborators listed in the Acknowledgments.

Notice of rights

Trademarks

Table of Contents

About The Art of Service

The Art of Service, Business Process Architects since 2000, is dedicated to helping stakeholders achieve excellence.

Defining, designing, creating, and implementing a process to solve a stakeholders challenge or meet an objective is the most valuable role… In EVERY group, company, organization and department.

Unless you're talking a one-time, single-use project, there should be a process. Whether that process is managed and implemented by humans, AI, or a combination of the two, it needs to be designed by someone with a complex enough perspective to ask the right questions.

Someone capable of asking the right questions and step back and say, 'What are we really trying to accomplish here? And is there a different way to look at it?'

With The Art of Service's Standard Requirements Self-Assessments, we empower people who can do just that — whether their title is marketer, entrepreneur, manager, salesperson, consultant, Business Process Manager, executive assistant, IT Manager, CIO etc... —they are the people who rule the future. They are people who watch the process as it happens, and ask the right questions to make the process work better.

Contact us when you need any support with this Self-Assessment and any help with templates, blue-prints and examples of standard documents you might need:

http://theartofservice.com
service@theartofservice.com

Included Resources - how to access

Included with your purchase of the book is the Privacy Risk

Self-Assessment Spreadsheet Dashboard which contains all questions and Self-Assessment areas and auto-generates insights, graphs, and project RACI planning - all with examples to get you started right away.

How? Simply send an email to
access@theartofservice.com
with this books' title in the subject to get the Privacy Risk Self Assessment Tool right away.

You will receive the following contents with New and Updated specific criteria:

- The latest quick edition of the book in PDF

- The latest complete edition of the book in PDF, which criteria correspond to the criteria in...

- The Self-Assessment Excel Dashboard, and...

- Example pre-filled Self-Assessment Excel Dashboard to get familiar with results generation

- In-depth specific Checklists covering the topic

- Project management checklists and templates to assist with implementation

INCLUDES LIFETIME SELF ASSESSMENT UPDATES

Every self assessment comes with Lifetime Updates and Lifetime Free Updated Books. Lifetime Updates is an industry-first feature which allows you to receive verified self assessment updates, ensuring you always have the most accurate information at your fingertips.

Get it now- you will be glad you did - do it now, before you forget.

Send an email to **access@theartofservice.com** with this books' title in the subject to get the Privacy Risk Self Assessment Tool right away.

Purpose of this Self-Assessment

This Self-Assessment has been developed to improve understanding of the requirements and elements of Privacy Risk, based on best practices and standards in business process architecture, design and quality management.

It is designed to allow for a rapid Self-Assessment to determine how closely existing management practices and procedures correspond to the elements of the Self-Assessment.

The criteria of requirements and elements of Privacy Risk have been rephrased in the format of a Self-Assessment questionnaire, with a seven-criterion scoring system, as explained in this document.

In this format, even with limited background knowledge of Privacy Risk, a manager can quickly review existing operations to determine how they measure up to the standards. This in turn can serve as the starting point of a 'gap analysis' to identify management tools or system elements that might usefully be implemented in the organization to help improve overall performance.

How to use the Self-Assessment

On the following pages are a series of questions to identify to what extent your Privacy Risk initiative is complete in comparison to the requirements set in standards.

To facilitate answering the questions, there is a space in front of each question to enter a score on a scale of '1' to '5'.

1 Strongly Disagree

2 Disagree

3 Neutral

4 Agree

5 Strongly Agree

Read the question and rate it with the following in front of mind:

'In my belief, the answer to this question is clearly defined'.

There are two ways in which you can choose to interpret this statement;
1. how aware are you that the answer to the question is clearly defined
2. for more in-depth analysis you can choose to gather evidence and confirm the answer to the question. This obviously will take more time, most Self-Assessment users opt for the first way to interpret the question and dig deeper later on based on the outcome of the overall Self-Assessment.

A score of '1' would mean that the answer is not clear at all, where a '5' would mean the answer is crystal clear and defined. Leave emtpy when the question is not applicable or you don't want to answer it, you can skip it without affecting your score. Write your score in the space provided.

After you have responded to all the appropriate statements in each section, compute your average score for that section, using the formula provided, and round to the nearest tenth. Then transfer to the corresponding spoke in the Privacy Risk Scorecard on the second next page of the Self-Assessment.

Your completed Privacy Risk Scorecard will give you a clear presentation of which Privacy Risk areas need attention.

Privacy Risk
Scorecard Example

Example of how the finalized Scorecard can look like:

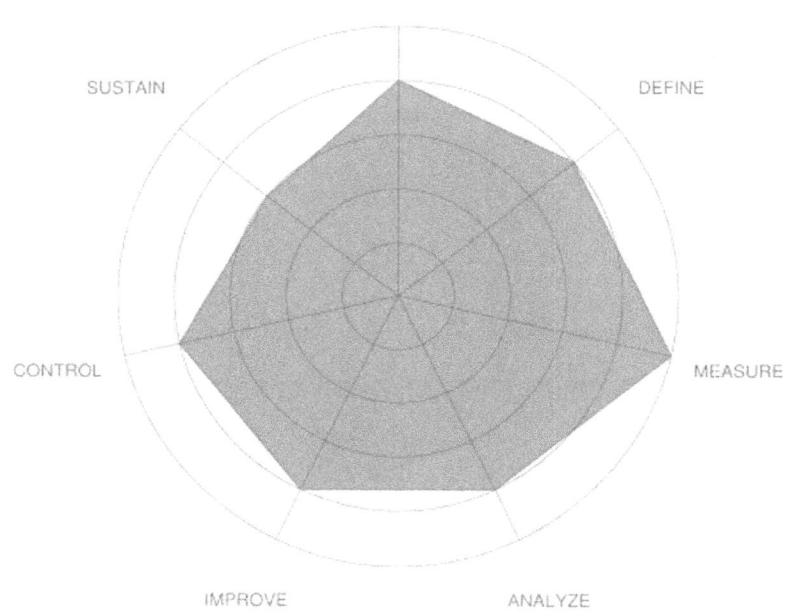

Privacy Risk Scorecard

Your Scores:

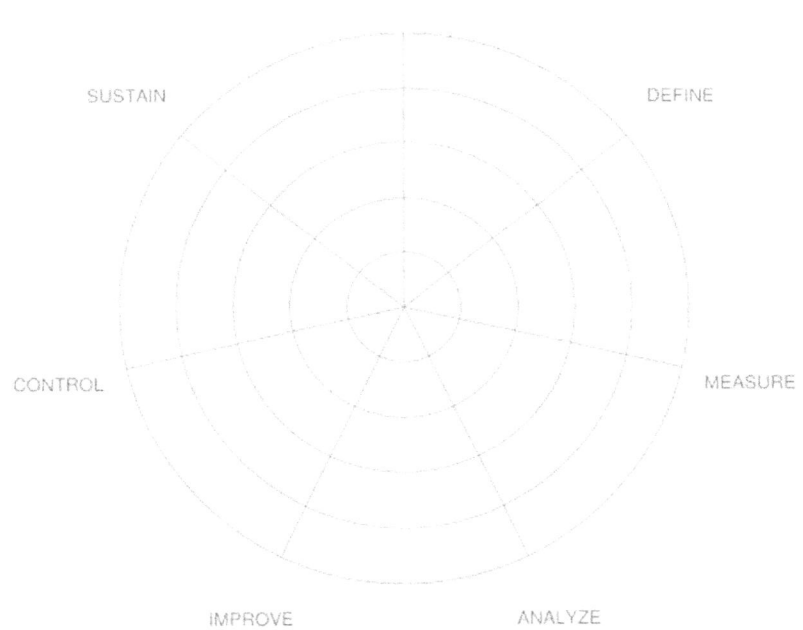

BEGINNING OF THE SELF-ASSESSMENT:

CRITERION #1: RECOGNIZE

INTENT: Be aware of the need for change. Recognize that there is an unfavorable variation, problem or symptom.

In my belief, the answer to this question is clearly defined:

5 Strongly Agree

4 Agree

3 Neutral

2 Disagree

1 Strongly Disagree

1. Where do you need to exercise leadership?
<--- Score

2. What privacy risk capabilities do you need?
<--- Score

3. Will a response program recognize when a crisis occurs and provide some level of response?
<--- Score

4. What information do users need?
<--- Score

5. Does privacy risk create potential expectations in other areas that need to be recognized and considered?
<--- Score

6. Which needs are not included or involved?
<--- Score

7. Looking at each person individually – does every one have the qualities which are needed to work in this group?
<--- Score

8. What prevents you from making the changes you know will make you a more effective privacy risk leader?
<--- Score

9. Why the need?
<--- Score

10. What else needs to be measured?
<--- Score

11. Is the quality assurance team identified?
<--- Score

12. What are the timeframes required to resolve each of the issues/problems?
<--- Score

13. What are the privacy risk resources needed?

<--- Score

14. What should be considered when identifying available resources, constraints, and deadlines?
<--- Score

15. What are the expected benefits of privacy risk to the stakeholder?
<--- Score

16. What creative shifts do you need to take?
<--- Score

17. What are the minority interests and what amount of minority interests can be recognized?
<--- Score

18. What is the recognized need?
<--- Score

19. What do employees need in the short term?
<--- Score

20. Are losses recognized in a timely manner?
<--- Score

21. What problems are you facing and how do you consider privacy risk will circumvent those obstacles?
<--- Score

22. How many trainings, in total, are needed?
<--- Score

23. What situation(s) led to this privacy risk Self Assessment?
<--- Score

24. For your privacy risk project, identify and describe the business environment, is there more than one layer to the business environment?
<--- Score

25. Where is training needed?
<--- Score

26. Will new equipment/products be required to facilitate privacy risk delivery, for example is new software needed?
<--- Score

27. Are there recognized privacy risk problems?
<--- Score

28. How do you recognize an privacy risk objection?
<--- Score

29. What is the problem or issue?
<--- Score

30. Who else hopes to benefit from it?
<--- Score

31. How do you identify the kinds of information that you will need?
<--- Score

32. Do you have/need 24-hour access to key personnel?
<--- Score

33. Does your organization need more privacy risk education?

<--- Score

34. What needs to stay?
<--- Score

35. Who should resolve the privacy risk issues?
<--- Score

36. Does the problem have ethical dimensions?
<--- Score

37. Are there any specific expectations or concerns about the privacy risk team, privacy risk itself?
<--- Score

38. As a sponsor, customer or management, how important is it to meet goals, objectives?
<--- Score

39. Who needs budgets?
<--- Score

40. How do you assess your privacy risk workforce capability and capacity needs, including skills, competencies, and staffing levels?
<--- Score

41. Are there any revenue recognition issues?
<--- Score

42. How much are sponsors, customers, partners, stakeholders involved in privacy risk? In other words, what are the risks, if privacy risk does not deliver successfully?
<--- Score

43. What privacy risk problem should be solved?
<--- Score

44. Who needs what information?
<--- Score

45. Will privacy risk deliverables need to be tested and, if so, by whom?
<--- Score

46. What activities does the governance board need to consider?
<--- Score

47. Who are your key stakeholders who need to sign off?
<--- Score

48. Are there privacy risk problems defined?
<--- Score

49. Can management personnel recognize the monetary benefit of privacy risk?
<--- Score

50. Is the need for organizational change recognized?
<--- Score

51. What resources or support might you need?
<--- Score

52. Did you miss any major privacy risk issues?
<--- Score

53. Are your goals realistic? Do you need to redefine your problem? Perhaps the problem has changed or

maybe you have reached your goal and need to set a new one?
<--- Score

54. Are there regulatory / compliance issues?
<--- Score

55. Which issues are too important to ignore?
<--- Score

56. What does privacy risk success mean to the stakeholders?
<--- Score

57. Do you need to avoid or amend any privacy risk activities?
<--- Score

58. Do you need different information or graphics?
<--- Score

59. How does it fit into your organizational needs and tasks?
<--- Score

60. Would you recognize a threat from the inside?
<--- Score

61. Think about the people you identified for your privacy risk project and the project responsibilities you would assign to them, what kind of training do you think they would need to perform these responsibilities effectively?
<--- Score

62. Will it solve real problems?

<--- Score

63. What is the privacy risk problem definition? What do you need to resolve?
<--- Score

64. What is the problem and/or vulnerability?
<--- Score

65. How do you recognize an objection?
<--- Score

66. How do you take a forward-looking perspective in identifying privacy risk research related to market response and models?
<--- Score

67. Do you recognize privacy risk achievements?
<--- Score

68. What is the smallest subset of the problem you can usefully solve?
<--- Score

69. Are controls defined to recognize and contain problems?
<--- Score

70. To what extent does each concerned units management team recognize privacy risk as an effective investment?
<--- Score

71. How are training requirements identified?
<--- Score

72. Which information does the privacy risk business case need to include?
<--- Score

73. What are your needs in relation to privacy risk skills, labor, equipment, and markets?
<--- Score

74. Are problem definition and motivation clearly presented?
<--- Score

75. Consider your own privacy risk project, what types of organizational problems do you think might be causing or affecting your problem, based on the work done so far?
<--- Score

76. What privacy risk events should you attend?
<--- Score

77. What would happen if privacy risk weren't done?
<--- Score

78. Are employees recognized or rewarded for performance that demonstrates the highest levels of integrity?
<--- Score

79. When a privacy risk manager recognizes a problem, what options are available?
<--- Score

80. To what extent would your organization benefit from being recognized as a award recipient?
<--- Score

81. Why is this needed?
<--- Score

82. What do you need to start doing?
<--- Score

83. How can auditing be a preventative security measure?
<--- Score

84. Is it clear when you think of the day ahead of you what activities and tasks you need to complete?
<--- Score

85. What training and capacity building actions are needed to implement proposed reforms?
<--- Score

86. How are the privacy risk's objectives aligned to the group's overall stakeholder strategy?
<--- Score

87. Who needs to know?
<--- Score

88. How do you identify subcontractor relationships?
<--- Score

89. Who needs to know about privacy risk?
<--- Score

90. What are the clients issues and concerns?
<--- Score

91. How are you going to measure success?

<--- Score

92. What are the stakeholder objectives to be achieved with privacy risk?
<--- Score

93. Are you dealing with any of the same issues today as yesterday? What can you do about this?
<--- Score

94. What privacy risk coordination do you need?
<--- Score

95. What needs to be done?
<--- Score

Add up total points for this section:
_ _ _ _ _ = Total points for this section

Divided by: _ _ _ _ _ _ (number of statements answered) = _ _ _ _ _ _
Average score for this section

Transfer your score to the privacy risk Index at the beginning of the Self-Assessment.

CRITERION #2: DEFINE:

1. What are the privacy risk tasks and definitions?
<--- Score

2. How are consistent privacy risk definitions important?
<--- Score

3. Is there a completed SIPOC representation, describing the Suppliers, Inputs, Process, Outputs, and

Customers?
<--- Score

4. How does the privacy risk manager ensure against scope creep?
<--- Score

5. Does the scope remain the same?
<--- Score

6. How did the privacy risk manager receive input to the development of a privacy risk improvement plan and the estimated completion dates/times of each activity?
<--- Score

7. Who defines (or who defined) the rules and roles?
<--- Score

8. Is there any additional privacy risk definition of success?
<--- Score

9. What defines best in class?
<--- Score

10. What is the scope of the privacy risk work?
<--- Score

11. How was the 'as is' process map developed, reviewed, verified and validated?
<--- Score

12. Are the privacy risk requirements complete?
<--- Score

13. What is out of scope?
<--- Score

14. How do you manage changes in privacy risk requirements?
<--- Score

15. What are (control) requirements for privacy risk Information?
<--- Score

16. Is privacy risk linked to key stakeholder goals and objectives?
<--- Score

17. What is the scope of privacy risk?
<--- Score

18. What is the worst case scenario?
<--- Score

19. Is the privacy risk scope manageable?
<--- Score

20. How can the value of privacy risk be defined?
<--- Score

21. Will a privacy risk production readiness review be required?
<--- Score

22. If substitutes have been appointed, have they been briefed on the privacy risk goals and received regular communications as to the progress to date?
<--- Score

23. Who approved the privacy risk scope?
<--- Score

24. Has the privacy risk work been fairly and/or equitably divided and delegated among team members who are qualified and capable to perform the work? Has everyone contributed?
<--- Score

25. What is the definition of privacy risk excellence?
<--- Score

26. Are different versions of process maps needed to account for the different types of inputs?
<--- Score

27. Is scope creep really all bad news?
<--- Score

28. How would you define privacy risk leadership?
<--- Score

29. Is data collected and displayed to better understand customer(s) critical needs and requirements.
<--- Score

30. Has a team charter been developed and communicated?
<--- Score

31. Have all basic functions of privacy risk been defined?
<--- Score

32. What are the compelling stakeholder reasons for

embarking on privacy risk?
<--- Score

33. How do you manage scope?
<--- Score

34. Why are you doing privacy risk and what is the scope?
<--- Score

35. Do you all define privacy risk in the same way?
<--- Score

36. Are accountability and ownership for privacy risk clearly defined?
<--- Score

37. Are required metrics defined, what are they?
<--- Score

38. What are the requirements for audit information?
<--- Score

39. Are resources adequate for the scope?
<--- Score

40. Are all requirements met?
<--- Score

41. What are the record-keeping requirements of privacy risk activities?
<--- Score

42. What specifically is the problem? Where does it occur? When does it occur? What is its extent?
<--- Score

43. The political context: who holds power?
<--- Score

44. What sources do you use to gather information for a privacy risk study?
<--- Score

45. What would be the goal or target for a privacy risk's improvement team?
<--- Score

46. What is the definition of success?
<--- Score

47. What was the context?
<--- Score

48. Has the direction changed at all during the course of privacy risk? If so, when did it change and why?
<--- Score

49. What information do you gather?
<--- Score

50. Has a high-level 'as is' process map been completed, verified and validated?
<--- Score

51. How do you hand over privacy risk context?
<--- Score

52. What are the core elements of the privacy risk business case?
<--- Score

53. What are the tasks and definitions?
<--- Score

54. Is there regularly 100% attendance at the team meetings? If not, have appointed substitutes attended to preserve cross-functionality and full representation?
<--- Score

55. What information should you gather?
<--- Score

56. Is the scope of privacy risk defined?
<--- Score

57. Who is gathering information?
<--- Score

58. Is there a completed, verified, and validated high-level 'as is' (not 'should be' or 'could be') stakeholder process map?
<--- Score

59. Where can you gather more information?
<--- Score

60. Is the work to date meeting requirements?
<--- Score

61. What are the privacy risk use cases?
<--- Score

62. How do you manage unclear privacy risk requirements?
<--- Score

63. Have specific policy objectives been defined?
<--- Score

64. What gets examined?
<--- Score

65. What sort of initial information to gather?
<--- Score

66. How do you gather privacy risk requirements?
<--- Score

67. What baselines are required to be defined and managed?
<--- Score

68. What critical content must be communicated – who, what, when, where, and how?
<--- Score

69. Have all of the relationships been defined properly?
<--- Score

70. When is the estimated completion date?
<--- Score

71. Are roles and responsibilities formally defined?
<--- Score

72. Is it clearly defined in and to your organization what you do?
<--- Score

73. Is the improvement team aware of the different versions of a process: what they think it is vs. what it

actually is vs. what it should be vs. what it could be?
<--- Score

74. Is the team adequately staffed with the desired cross-functionality? If not, what additional resources are available to the team?
<--- Score

75. When is/was the privacy risk start date?
<--- Score

76. Has a project plan, Gantt chart, or similar been developed/completed?
<--- Score

77. Have the customer needs been translated into specific, measurable requirements? How?
<--- Score

78. Scope of sensitive information?
<--- Score

79. Is privacy risk currently on schedule according to the plan?
<--- Score

80. Has the improvement team collected the 'voice of the customer' (obtained feedback – qualitative and quantitative)?
<--- Score

81. How would you define the culture at your organization, how susceptible is it to privacy risk changes?
<--- Score

82. Is the privacy risk scope complete and appropriately sized?
<--- Score

83. Has everyone on the team, including the team leaders, been properly trained?
<--- Score

84. When are meeting minutes sent out? Who is on the distribution list?
<--- Score

85. Is the team equipped with available and reliable resources?
<--- Score

86. What is in scope?
<--- Score

87. What customer feedback methods were used to solicit their input?
<--- Score

88. Who is gathering privacy risk information?
<--- Score

89. Is privacy risk required?
<--- Score

90. Does the team have regular meetings?
<--- Score

91. What are the Roles and Responsibilities for each team member and its leadership? Where is this documented?
<--- Score

92. What privacy risk requirements should be gathered?
<--- Score

93. Are there any constraints known that bear on the ability to perform privacy risk work? How is the team addressing them?
<--- Score

94. What is in the scope and what is not in scope?
<--- Score

95. Are task requirements clearly defined?
<--- Score

96. How do you think the partners involved in privacy risk would have defined success?
<--- Score

97. What is the scope of the privacy risk effort?
<--- Score

98. What is the context?
<--- Score

99. How will variation in the actual durations of each activity be dealt with to ensure that the expected privacy risk results are met?
<--- Score

100. How do you keep key subject matter experts in the loop?
<--- Score

101. Has/have the customer(s) been identified?

<--- Score

102. Do you have a privacy risk success story or case study ready to tell and share?
<--- Score

103. How often are the team meetings?
<--- Score

104. Has anyone else (internal or external to the group) attempted to solve this problem or a similar one before? If so, what knowledge can be leveraged from these previous efforts?
<--- Score

105. What is a worst-case scenario for losses?
<--- Score

106. Are there different segments of customers?
<--- Score

107. What key stakeholder process output measure(s) does privacy risk leverage and how?
<--- Score

108. How do you build the right business case?
<--- Score

109. Is there a critical path to deliver privacy risk results?
<--- Score

110. What scope do you want your strategy to cover?
<--- Score

111. How will the privacy risk team and the group

measure complete success of privacy risk?

<--- Score

112. What are the boundaries of the scope? What is in bounds and what is not? What is the start point? What is the stop point?

<--- Score

113. Who are the privacy risk improvement team members, including Management Leads and Coaches?

<--- Score

114. Are audit criteria, scope, frequency and methods defined?

<--- Score

115. What system do you use for gathering privacy risk information?

<--- Score

116. Is there a privacy risk management charter, including stakeholder case, problem and goal statements, scope, milestones, roles and responsibilities, communication plan?

<--- Score

117. In what way can you redefine the criteria of choice clients have in your category in your favor?

<--- Score

118. Is special privacy risk user knowledge required?

<--- Score

119. Is there a clear privacy risk case definition?

<--- Score

120. How do you gather the stories?
<--- Score

121. How do you catch privacy risk definition inconsistencies?
<--- Score

122. What constraints exist that might impact the team?
<--- Score

123. Are customer(s) identified and segmented according to their different needs and requirements?
<--- Score

124. What happens if privacy risk's scope changes?
<--- Score

125. What are the dynamics of the communication plan?
<--- Score

126. How is the team tracking and documenting its work?
<--- Score

127. Are approval levels defined for contracts and supplements to contracts?
<--- Score

128. Has a privacy risk requirement not been met?
<--- Score

129. Has your scope been defined?
<--- Score

130. What are the rough order estimates on cost savings/opportunities that privacy risk brings?
<--- Score

131. Do the problem and goal statements meet the SMART criteria (specific, measurable, attainable, relevant, and time-bound)?
<--- Score

132. What is out-of-scope initially?
<--- Score

133. Is the current 'as is' process being followed? If not, what are the discrepancies?
<--- Score

134. How do you gather requirements?
<--- Score

135. Do you have organizational privacy requirements?
<--- Score

136. What knowledge or experience is required?
<--- Score

Add up total points for this section:
_ _ _ _ _ = Total points for this section

Divided by: _ _ _ _ _ _ (number of statements answered) = _ _ _ _ _ _
Average score for this section

Transfer your score to the privacy risk Index at the beginning of the Self-

Assessment.

CRITERION #3: MEASURE:

INTENT: Gather the correct data. Measure the current performance and evolution of the situation.

In my belief, the answer to this question is clearly defined:

5 Strongly Agree

4 Agree

3 Neutral

2 Disagree

1 Strongly Disagree

1. What does verifying compliance entail?
<--- Score

2. What are the types and number of measures to use?
<--- Score

3. How will success or failure be measured?
<--- Score

4. What could cause you to change course?
<--- Score

5. Which measures and indicators matter?
<--- Score

6. Who pays the cost?
<--- Score

7. What causes mismanagement?
<--- Score

8. Have you made assumptions about the shape of the future, particularly its impact on your customers and competitors?
<--- Score

9. What details are required of the privacy risk cost structure?
<--- Score

10. What are the current costs of the privacy risk process?
<--- Score

11. Does a privacy risk quantification method exist?
<--- Score

12. How can a privacy risk test verify your ideas or assumptions?
<--- Score

13. Do you verify that corrective actions were taken?
<--- Score

14. What are hidden privacy risk quality costs?

<--- Score

15. Why do the measurements/indicators matter?
<--- Score

16. How do you verify the privacy risk requirements quality?
<--- Score

17. Will privacy risk have an impact on current business continuity, disaster recovery processes and/or infrastructure?
<--- Score

18. How will you measure your privacy risk effectiveness?
<--- Score

19. How will costs be allocated?
<--- Score

20. What are the privacy risk investment costs?
<--- Score

21. Where is it measured?
<--- Score

22. What are your customers expectations and measures?
<--- Score

23. When should you bother with diagrams?
<--- Score

24. What is the total cost related to deploying privacy risk, including any consulting or professional services?

<--- Score

25. Among the privacy risk product and service cost to be estimated, which is considered hardest to estimate?
<--- Score

26. Do you have a flow diagram of what happens?
<--- Score

27. What relevant entities could be measured?
<--- Score

28. What does your operating model cost?
<--- Score

29. What disadvantage does this cause for the user?
<--- Score

30. What methods are feasible and acceptable to estimate the impact of reforms?
<--- Score

31. What users will be impacted?
<--- Score

32. How do you aggregate measures across priorities?
<--- Score

33. How are costs allocated?
<--- Score

34. How can you reduce costs?
<--- Score

35. Do the benefits outweigh the costs?

<--- Score

36. Are the units of measure consistent?
<--- Score

37. How frequently do you track privacy risk measures?
<--- Score

38. What is the privacy risk business impact?
<--- Score

39. What does a Test Case verify?
<--- Score

40. What is the root cause(s) of the problem?
<--- Score

41. Is there an opportunity to verify requirements?
<--- Score

42. Are there measurements based on task performance?
<--- Score

43. What potential environmental factors impact the privacy risk effort?
<--- Score

44. How will measures be used to manage and adapt?
<--- Score

45. How sensitive must the privacy risk strategy be to cost?
<--- Score

46. What are the strategic priorities for this year?
<--- Score

47. How do you verify performance?
<--- Score

48. Are privacy risk vulnerabilities categorized and prioritized?
<--- Score

49. What are you verifying?
<--- Score

50. How do you verify your resources?
<--- Score

51. How are measurements made?
<--- Score

52. How is performance measured?
<--- Score

53. What are the operational costs after privacy risk deployment?
<--- Score

54. What are the costs and benefits?
<--- Score

55. What are the privacy risk key cost drivers?
<--- Score

56. How do you verify the authenticity of the data and information used?
<--- Score

57. Is it possible to estimate the impact of unanticipated complexity such as wrong or failed assumptions, feedback, etcetera on proposed reforms?
<--- Score

58. What tests verify requirements?
<--- Score

59. Why do you expend time and effort to implement measurement, for whom?
<--- Score

60. How can you reduce the costs of obtaining inputs?
<--- Score

61. How can you manage cost down?
<--- Score

62. Are supply costs steady or fluctuating?
<--- Score

63. What measurements are being captured?
<--- Score

64. Does the privacy risk task fit the client's priorities?
<--- Score

65. What causes extra work or rework?
<--- Score

66. Does management have the right priorities among projects?
<--- Score

67. Which costs should be taken into account?

<--- Score

68. Where can you go to verify the info?
<--- Score

69. Is the solution cost-effective?
<--- Score

70. What do people want to verify?
<--- Score

71. What would be a real cause for concern?
<--- Score

72. Have design-to-cost goals been established?
<--- Score

73. What would it cost to replace your technology?
<--- Score

74. How do you verify privacy risk completeness and accuracy?
<--- Score

75. Where is the cost?
<--- Score

76. Who should receive measurement reports?
<--- Score

77. Do you aggressively reward and promote the people who have the biggest impact on creating excellent privacy risk services/products?
<--- Score

78. Are the measurements objective?

<--- Score

79. What is an unallowable cost?
<--- Score

80. At what cost?
<--- Score

81. Who is involved in verifying compliance?
<--- Score

82. Are you taking your company in the direction of better and revenue or cheaper and cost?
<--- Score

83. Has a cost center been established?
<--- Score

84. What are your key privacy risk organizational performance measures, including key short and longer-term financial measures?
<--- Score

85. Are you able to realize any cost savings?
<--- Score

86. How do you control the overall costs of your work processes?
<--- Score

87. How will you measure success?
<--- Score

88. When are costs are incurred?
<--- Score

89. What evidence is there and what is measured?
<--- Score

90. What do you measure and why?
<--- Score

91. What causes innovation to fail or succeed in your organization?
<--- Score

92. Was a business case (cost/benefit) developed?
<--- Score

93. Do you have any cost privacy risk limitation requirements?
<--- Score

94. What are the costs?
<--- Score

95. How do you verify and develop ideas and innovations?
<--- Score

96. What causes investor action?
<--- Score

97. How do you quantify and qualify impacts?
<--- Score

98. How much does it cost?
<--- Score

99. Are actual costs in line with budgeted costs?
<--- Score

100. What measurements are possible, practicable and meaningful?
<--- Score

101. Is the cost worth the privacy risk effort ?
<--- Score

102. What is your decision requirements diagram?
<--- Score

103. What are the costs of delaying privacy risk action?
<--- Score

104. Did you tackle the cause or the symptom?
<--- Score

105. What can be used to verify compliance?
<--- Score

106. How is the value delivered by privacy risk being measured?
<--- Score

107. Are there any easy-to-implement alternatives to privacy risk? Sometimes other solutions are available that do not require the cost implications of a full-blown project?
<--- Score

108. How do you measure success?
<--- Score

109. How long to keep data and how to manage retention costs?
<--- Score

110. What does losing customers cost your organization?
<--- Score

111. What are the costs of reform?
<--- Score

112. How can you measure the performance?
<--- Score

113. What could cause delays in the schedule?
<--- Score

114. How will your organization measure success?
<--- Score

115. How do you measure lifecycle phases?
<--- Score

116. How will effects be measured?
<--- Score

117. What is your privacy risk quality cost segregation study?
<--- Score

118. What harm might be caused?
<--- Score

119. What drives O&M cost?
<--- Score

120. What is measured? Why?
<--- Score

121. What are the estimated costs of proposed

changes?
<--- Score

122. How do your measurements capture actionable privacy risk information for use in exceeding your customers expectations and securing your customers engagement?
<--- Score

123. Do you have an issue in getting priority?
<--- Score

124. When a disaster occurs, who gets priority?
<--- Score

125. What is the total fixed cost?
<--- Score

126. Are the privacy risk benefits worth its costs?
<--- Score

127. What is the cause of any privacy risk gaps?
<--- Score

128. What are your primary costs, revenues, assets?
<--- Score

129. Are missed privacy risk opportunities costing your organization money?
<--- Score

130. How do you prevent mis-estimating cost?
<--- Score

131. What happens if cost savings do not materialize?
<--- Score

Add up total points for this section:
_____ = Total points for this section

Divided by: _____ (number of
statements answered) = _____
Average score for this section

Transfer your score to the privacy risk
Index at the beginning of the Self-
Assessment.

CRITERION #4: ANALYZE:

INTENT: Analyze causes, assumptions and hypotheses.

In my belief, the answer to this question is clearly defined:

5 Strongly Agree

4 Agree

3 Neutral

2 Disagree

1 Strongly Disagree

1. Would the development of a framework for privacy risk management be an effective mechanism for addressing challenges with big data?
<--- Score

2. What are your current levels and trends in key measures or indicators of privacy risk product and process performance that are important to and directly serve your customers? How do these results

compare with the performance of your competitors and other organizations with similar offerings?
<--- Score

3. Which privacy risk data should be retained?
<--- Score

4. Are privacy risk changes recognized early enough to be approved through the regular process?
<--- Score

5. What are the best opportunities for value improvement?
<--- Score

6. What qualifications do privacy risk leaders need?
<--- Score

7. How do your work systems and key work processes relate to and capitalize on your core competencies?
<--- Score

8. What are the privacy risk business drivers?
<--- Score

9. What process improvements will be needed?
<--- Score

10. What are your current levels and trends in key privacy risk measures or indicators of product and process performance that are important to and directly serve your customers?
<--- Score

11. Who qualifies to gain access to data?
<--- Score

12. Who is involved with workflow mapping?
<--- Score

13. What other jobs or tasks affect the performance of the steps in the privacy risk process?
<--- Score

14. What are your outputs?
<--- Score

15. Do your employees have the opportunity to do what they do best everyday?
<--- Score

16. Do you, as a leader, bounce back quickly from setbacks?
<--- Score

17. What is the cost of poor quality as supported by the team's analysis?
<--- Score

18. What controls do you have in place to protect data?
<--- Score

19. Where is the data coming from to measure compliance?
<--- Score

20. What are evaluation criteria for the output?
<--- Score

21. What privacy risk data should be managed?
<--- Score

22. Do several people in different organizational units assist with the privacy risk process?
<--- Score

23. An organizationally feasible system request is one that considers the mission, goals and objectives of the organization, key questions are: is the privacy risk solution request practical and will it solve a problem or take advantage of an opportunity to achieve company goals?
<--- Score

24. What is your organizations system for selecting qualified vendors?
<--- Score

25. Were Pareto charts (or similar) used to portray the 'heavy hitters' (or key sources of variation)?
<--- Score

26. How do you identify specific privacy risk investment opportunities and emerging trends?
<--- Score

27. What qualifies as competition?
<--- Score

28. What did the team gain from developing a sub-process map?
<--- Score

29. How is data used for program management and improvement?
<--- Score

30. Do your contracts/agreements contain data security obligations?
<--- Score

31. What are the personnel training and qualifications required?
<--- Score

32. How is the data gathered?
<--- Score

33. Does the open data program evaluate privacy risk in light of relevant public records laws?
<--- Score

34. What will drive privacy risk change?
<--- Score

35. What internal processes need improvement?
<--- Score

36. Do quality systems drive continuous improvement?
<--- Score

37. What conclusions were drawn from the team's data collection and analysis? How did the team reach these conclusions?
<--- Score

38. Is there an established change management process?
<--- Score

39. How often will data be collected for measures?
<--- Score

40. Are all team members qualified for all tasks?
<--- Score

41. Is pre-qualification of suppliers carried out?
<--- Score

42. Can you add value to the current privacy risk decision-making process (largely qualitative) by incorporating uncertainty modeling (more quantitative)?
<--- Score

43. What are the privacy risk design outputs?
<--- Score

44. How is the way you as the leader think and process information affecting your organizational culture?
<--- Score

45. What are your key performance measures or indicators and in-process measures for the control and improvement of your privacy risk processes?
<--- Score

46. Is the privacy risk process severely broken such that a re-design is necessary?
<--- Score

47. How will the change process be managed?
<--- Score

48. What qualifications and skills do you need?
<--- Score

49. How many input/output points does it require?

<--- Score

50. Was a detailed process map created to amplify critical steps of the 'as is' stakeholder process?
<--- Score

51. What are the disruptive privacy risk technologies that enable your organization to radically change your business processes?
<--- Score

52. How do mission and objectives affect the privacy risk processes of your organization?
<--- Score

53. How are outputs preserved and protected?
<--- Score

54. Have you defined which data is gathered how?
<--- Score

55. What other organizational variables, such as reward systems or communication systems, affect the performance of this privacy risk process?
<--- Score

56. Has data output been validated?
<--- Score

57. What privacy risk data do you gather or use now?
<--- Score

58. Is the required privacy risk data gathered?
<--- Score

59. Who is involved in the management review

process?

<--- Score

60. Who will facilitate the team and process?

<--- Score

61. Were any designed experiments used to generate additional insight into the data analysis?

<--- Score

62. Was a cause-and-effect diagram used to explore the different types of causes (or sources of variation)?

<--- Score

63. What output to create?

<--- Score

64. Who gets your output?

<--- Score

65. Has an output goal been set?

<--- Score

66. How is the privacy risk Value Stream Mapping managed?

<--- Score

67. How do you use privacy risk data and information to support organizational decision making and innovation?

<--- Score

68. Is the suppliers process defined and controlled?

<--- Score

69. What data is gathered?

<--- Score

70. What is your organizations process which leads to recognition of value generation?
<--- Score

71. What does the data say about the performance of the stakeholder process?
<--- Score

72. What were the crucial 'moments of truth' on the process map?
<--- Score

73. What training and qualifications will you need?
<--- Score

74. What are your best practices for minimizing privacy risk project risk, while demonstrating incremental value and quick wins throughout the privacy risk project lifecycle?
<--- Score

75. Would the development of a framework for privacy risk management be an effective mechanism for addressing the challenges of big data?
<--- Score

76. What privacy risks are associated with the collection, use, dissemination and maintenance of the data?
<--- Score

77. Do your leaders quickly bounce back from setbacks?

<--- Score

78. Is the final output clearly identified?
<--- Score

79. What are the processes for audit reporting and management?
<--- Score

80. What is the output?
<--- Score

81. How will corresponding data be collected?
<--- Score

82. What privacy risk data will be collected?
<--- Score

83. What data do you need to collect?
<--- Score

84. What were the financial benefits resulting from any 'ground fruit or low-hanging fruit' (quick fixes)?
<--- Score

85. What tools were used to narrow the list of possible causes?
<--- Score

86. Do you understand your management processes today?
<--- Score

87. Record-keeping requirements flow from the records needed as inputs, outputs, controls and for transformation of a privacy risk process, are the

records needed as inputs to the privacy risk process available?

<--- Score

88. Are all staff in core privacy risk subjects Highly Qualified?

<--- Score

89. What is the privacy risk Driver?

<--- Score

90. How will the data be checked for quality?

<--- Score

91. Identify an operational issue in your organization, for example, could a particular task be done more quickly or more efficiently by privacy risk?

<--- Score

92. What successful thing are you doing today that may be blinding you to new growth opportunities?

<--- Score

93. Where can you get qualified talent today?

<--- Score

94. Are you missing privacy risk opportunities?

<--- Score

95. What types of data do your privacy risk indicators require?

<--- Score

96. How can risk management be tied procedurally to process elements?

<--- Score

97. How do you promote understanding that opportunity for improvement is not criticism of the status quo, or the people who created the status quo?
<--- Score

98. What information qualified as important?
<--- Score

99. What systems/processes must you excel at?
<--- Score

100. Are your outputs consistent?
<--- Score

101. Were there any improvement opportunities identified from the process analysis?
<--- Score

102. How do you define collaboration and team output?
<--- Score

103. Do staff qualifications match your project?
<--- Score

104. How difficult is it to qualify what privacy risk ROI is?
<--- Score

105. What resources go in to get the desired output?
<--- Score

106. What is the Value Stream Mapping?
<--- Score

107. What qualifications are necessary?
<--- Score

108. Do you have the authority to produce the output?
<--- Score

109. What kind of crime could a potential new hire have committed that would not only not disqualify him/her from being hired by your organization, but would actually indicate that he/she might be a particularly good fit?
<--- Score

110. Where is privacy risk data gathered?
<--- Score

111. What quality tools were used to get through the analyze phase?
<--- Score

112. How much data can be collected in the given timeframe?
<--- Score

113. Does the open data program engage and educate the public about the privacy risks of open data?
<--- Score

114. How do you ensure that the privacy risk opportunity is realistic?
<--- Score

115. What is the complexity of the output produced?
<--- Score

116. How does the organization define, manage, and improve its privacy risk processes?
<--- Score

117. What methods do you use to gather privacy risk data?
<--- Score

118. What do you need to qualify?
<--- Score

119. What are the revised rough estimates of the financial savings/opportunity for privacy risk improvements?
<--- Score

120. What process should you select for improvement?
<--- Score

121. What is the perception among users of potential security and privacy risks associated with using cloud data storage solutions?
<--- Score

122. Is there any way to speed up the process?
<--- Score

123. A compounding model resolution with available relevant data can often provide insight towards a solution methodology; which privacy risk models, tools and techniques are necessary?
<--- Score

124. What tools were used to generate the list of

possible causes?
<--- Score

125. When should a process be art not science?
<--- Score

126. What qualifications are needed?
<--- Score

127. Think about the functions involved in your privacy risk project, what processes flow from these functions?
<--- Score

128. What are your privacy risk processes?
<--- Score

129. Is there a strict change management process?
<--- Score

130. What privacy risk metrics are outputs of the process?
<--- Score

Add up total points for this section:
_ _ _ _ _ = Total points for this section

Divided by: _ _ _ _ _ _ (number of statements answered) = _ _ _ _ _ _
Average score for this section

Transfer your score to the privacy risk Index at the beginning of the Self-Assessment.

CRITERION #5: IMPROVE:

INTENT: Develop a practical solution.
Innovate, establish and test the
solution and to measure the results.

In my belief, the answer to this
question is clearly defined:

5 Strongly Agree

4 Agree

3 Neutral

2 Disagree

1 Strongly Disagree

1. What alternative responses are available to manage
risk?
<--- Score

2. How can you improve privacy risk?
<--- Score

**3. Is identifying and assessing security and privacy
risks a part of the overall risk management**

effort for each system supporting or part of this investment?
<--- Score

4. Who will be responsible for making the decisions to include or exclude requested changes once privacy risk is underway?
<--- Score

5. Is the measure of success for privacy risk understandable to a variety of people?
<--- Score

6. Will the controls trigger any other risks?
<--- Score

7. Who are the privacy risk decision-makers?
<--- Score

8. How is knowledge sharing about risk management improved?
<--- Score

9. Who manages privacy risk risk?
<--- Score

10. How will you know when its improved?
<--- Score

11. Risk Identification: What are the possible risk events your organization faces in relation to privacy risk?
<--- Score

12. What laws & regulations govern Cyber and Privacy risks?

<--- Score

13. When you map the key players in your own work and the types/domains of relationships with them, which relationships do you find easy and which challenging, and why?
<--- Score

14. Can you identify any significant risks or exposures to privacy risk third- parties (vendors, service providers, alliance partners etc) that concern you?
<--- Score

15. At what point will vulnerability assessments be performed once privacy risk is put into production (e.g., ongoing Risk Management after implementation)?
<--- Score

16. How does the team improve its work?
<--- Score

17. Do vendor agreements bring new compliance risk ?
<--- Score

18. What actually has to improve and by how much?
<--- Score

19. How will you measure the results?
<--- Score

20. Considering the type of information collected and sources of collection, what privacy risks were identified and how were corresponding risks mitigated?

<--- Score

21. How does your organization evaluate strategic privacy risk success?
<--- Score

22. How will you know that a change is an improvement?
<--- Score

23. What area needs the greatest improvement?
<--- Score

24. How do you measure risk?
<--- Score

25. Is the scope clearly documented?
<--- Score

26. What are the expected privacy risk results?
<--- Score

27. Are the most efficient solutions problem-specific?
<--- Score

28. How do you deal with privacy risk risk?
<--- Score

29. How do you keep improving privacy risk?
<--- Score

30. How do you conduct a privacy risk assessment?
<--- Score

31. Where do the privacy risk decisions reside?
<--- Score

32. What criteria will you use to assess your privacy risk risks?
<--- Score

33. What should a proof of concept or pilot accomplish?
<--- Score

34. Is the privacy risk risk managed?
<--- Score

35. Have you achieved privacy risk improvements?
<--- Score

36. Explorations of the frontiers of privacy risk will help you build influence, improve privacy risk, optimize decision making, and sustain change, what is your approach?
<--- Score

37. What tools do you use once you have decided on a privacy risk strategy and more importantly how do you choose?
<--- Score

38. Who manages supplier risk management in your organization?
<--- Score

39. What are the affordable privacy risk risks?
<--- Score

40. Who are the privacy risk decision makers?
<--- Score

41. How can you better manage risk?
<--- Score

42. How do you promote an integrated approach to risk management?
<--- Score

43. How do you go about comparing privacy risk approaches/solutions?
<--- Score

44. Is the privacy risk solution sustainable?
<--- Score

45. For estimation problems, how do you develop an estimation statement?
<--- Score

46. Is privacy risk documentation maintained?
<--- Score

47. Is risk periodically assessed?
<--- Score

48. How do you link measurement and risk?
<--- Score

49. Have you identified breakpoints and/or risk tolerances that will trigger broad consideration of a potential need for intervention or modification of strategy?
<--- Score

50. How significant is the improvement in the eyes of the end user?
<--- Score

51. Does a good decision guarantee a good outcome?
<--- Score

52. How do you mitigate privacy risk risk?
<--- Score

53. How are privacy risk risks managed?
<--- Score

54. Who has approved the privacy risks involved in the project?
<--- Score

55. What is the privacy risk's sustainability risk?
<--- Score

56. How do you evaluate security and privacy risk?
<--- Score

57. How can you improve performance?
<--- Score

58. What is the risk?
<--- Score

59. Is the privacy risk documentation thorough?
<--- Score

60. Are you assessing privacy risk and risk?
<--- Score

61. What are the objectives in assessing privacy risk in a transitive health information workflow?
<--- Score

62. How do you measure progress and evaluate training effectiveness?
<--- Score

63. Does the goal represent a desired result that can be measured?
<--- Score

64. What to do with the results or outcomes of measurements?
<--- Score

65. What are the concrete privacy risk results?
<--- Score

66. What are the privacy risks associated with this system and how are those risks mitigated?
<--- Score

67. Explain what practical steps you will take to ensure that you identify and address privacy risks. Who should be consulted internally and externally?
<--- Score

68. What risks do you need to manage?
<--- Score

69. The distribution of privacy risks: who needs protection?
<--- Score

70. Risk events: what are the things that could go wrong?
<--- Score

71. Is supporting privacy risk documentation required?
<--- Score

72. How do insurance carriers price cyber and privacy risks?
<--- Score

73. Is there any other privacy risk solution?
<--- Score

74. How do you decide how much to remunerate an employee?
<--- Score

75. What is privacy risk risk?
<--- Score

76. What people should be consulted on privacy risks?
<--- Score

77. How do you improve privacy risk service perception, and satisfaction?
<--- Score

78. Which privacy risk solution is appropriate?
<--- Score

79. What improvements have been achieved?
<--- Score

80. What privacy risk improvements can be made?
<--- Score

81. Who controls key decisions that will be made?

<--- Score

82. What current systems have to be understood and/
or changed?
<--- Score

83. Are risk management tasks balanced centrally and
locally?
<--- Score

84. Where do you need privacy risk improvement?
<--- Score

85. Are the key business and technology risks being
managed?
<--- Score

86. How risky is your organization?
<--- Score

87. Who are the key stakeholders for the privacy risk
evaluation?
<--- Score

88. privacy risk risk decisions: whose call Is It?
<--- Score

89. Are procedures documented for managing privacy
risk risks?
<--- Score

90. How can the phases of privacy risk development
be identified?
<--- Score

91. How will you know that you have improved?

<--- Score

92. In the past few months, what is the smallest change you have made that has had the biggest positive result? What was it about that small change that produced the large return?
<--- Score

93. How do you define the solutions' scope?
<--- Score

94. Do you need to do a usability evaluation?
<--- Score

95. Are decisions made in a timely manner?
<--- Score

96. What needs improvement? Why?
<--- Score

97. How is continuous improvement applied to risk management?
<--- Score

98. Risk factors: what are the characteristics of privacy risk that make it risky?
<--- Score

99. Have done your due diligence when looking at privacy risk assessments?
<--- Score

100. Is there a high likelihood that any recommendations will achieve their intended results?
<--- Score

101. What do you want to improve?
<--- Score

102. Who will be responsible for documenting the privacy risk requirements in detail?
<--- Score

103. What were the criteria for evaluating a privacy risk pilot?
<--- Score

104. Who should make the privacy risk decisions?
<--- Score

105. Do you have the optimal project management team structure?
<--- Score

106. What are the implications of the one critical privacy risk decision 10 minutes, 10 months, and 10 years from now?
<--- Score

107. Who controls the risk?
<--- Score

108. Why improve in the first place?
<--- Score

109. Who makes the privacy risk decisions in your organization?
<--- Score

110. How do you improve productivity?
<--- Score

111. Can you integrate quality management and risk management?
<--- Score

112. What resources are required for the improvement efforts?
<--- Score

113. What went well, what should change, what can improve?
<--- Score

114. Are the risks fully understood, reasonable and manageable?
<--- Score

115. How are policy decisions made and where?
<--- Score

116. Do those selected for the privacy risk team have a good general understanding of what privacy risk is all about?
<--- Score

117. Who do you report privacy risk results to?
<--- Score

118. Which of the recognised risks out of all risks can be most likely transferred?
<--- Score

119. How scalable is your privacy risk solution?
<--- Score

120. How do you manage and improve your privacy risk work systems to deliver customer value and

achieve organizational success and sustainability?
<--- Score

121. How do the privacy risk results compare with the performance of your competitors and other organizations with similar offerings?
<--- Score

122. What practices helps your organization to develop its capacity to recognize patterns?
<--- Score

123. Are events managed to resolution?
<--- Score

124. How do you manage privacy risk risk?
<--- Score

125. How can skill-level changes improve privacy risk?
<--- Score

126. How will you recognize and celebrate results?
<--- Score

127. Do you cover the five essential competencies: Communication, Collaboration,Innovation, Adaptability, and Leadership that improve an organizations ability to leverage the new privacy risk in a volatile global economy?
<--- Score

128. What can you do to improve?
<--- Score

129. What assumptions are made about the solution and approach?

<--- Score

130. Is the solution technically practical?
<--- Score

131. Can the solution be designed and implemented within an acceptable time period?
<--- Score

132. What are the privacy risk security risks?
<--- Score

Add up total points for this section:
_____ = Total points for this section

Divided by: _____ (number of statements answered) = _____
Average score for this section

Transfer your score to the privacy risk Index at the beginning of the Self-Assessment.

CRITERION #6: CONTROL:

INTENT: Implement the practical solution. Maintain the performance and correct possible complications.

In my belief, the answer to this question is clearly defined:

5 Strongly Agree

4 Agree

3 Neutral

2 Disagree

1 Strongly Disagree

1. Is there documentation that will support the successful operation of the improvement?
<--- Score

2. Is there a transfer of ownership and knowledge to process owner and process team tasked with the responsibilities.
<--- Score

3. Are operating procedures consistent?
<--- Score

4. How do you plan on providing proper recognition and disclosure of supporting companies?
<--- Score

5. Is there an action plan in case of emergencies?
<--- Score

6. How do your controls stack up?
<--- Score

7. How will input, process, and output variables be checked to detect for sub-optimal conditions?
<--- Score

8. What are your results for key measures or indicators of the accomplishment of your privacy risk strategy and action plans, including building and strengthening core competencies?
<--- Score

9. How is privacy risk project cost planned, managed, monitored?
<--- Score

10. Is there a documented and implemented monitoring plan?
<--- Score

11. How can you best use all of your knowledge repositories to enhance learning and sharing?
<--- Score

12. Are there documented procedures?

<--- Score

13. Is there a standardized process?
<--- Score

14. Is there a privacy risk Communication plan covering who needs to get what information when?
<--- Score

15. How will the process owner and team be able to hold the gains?
<--- Score

16. What are the performance and scale of the privacy risk tools?
<--- Score

17. Are pertinent alerts monitored, analyzed and distributed to appropriate personnel?
<--- Score

18. How will privacy risk decisions be made and monitored?
<--- Score

19. What are the critical parameters to watch?
<--- Score

20. Do the privacy risk decisions you make today help people and the planet tomorrow?
<--- Score

21. Is there a control plan in place for sustaining improvements (short and long-term)?
<--- Score

22. What is your theory of human motivation, and how does your compensation plan fit with that view?
<--- Score

23. How will report readings be checked to effectively monitor performance?
<--- Score

24. What is the control/monitoring plan?
<--- Score

25. How do you spread information?
<--- Score

26. What is the best design framework for privacy risk organization now that, in a post industrial-age if the top-down, command and control model is no longer relevant?
<--- Score

27. Who is the privacy risk process owner?
<--- Score

28. What quality tools were useful in the control phase?
<--- Score

29. How do you plan for the cost of succession?
<--- Score

30. Is a response plan established and deployed?
<--- Score

31. What is the standard for acceptable privacy risk performance?
<--- Score

32. How do you establish and deploy modified action plans if circumstances require a shift in plans and rapid execution of new plans?
<--- Score

33. Do the viable solutions scale to future needs?
<--- Score

34. Has the improved process and its steps been standardized?
<--- Score

35. Are controls in place and consistently applied?
<--- Score

36. What are individuals protections against privacy risks?
<--- Score

37. Are identified privacy risks and associated mitigation plans formally documented and reviewed by management?
<--- Score

38. How will the day-to-day responsibilities for monitoring and continual improvement be transferred from the improvement team to the process owner?
<--- Score

39. What do your reports reflect?
<--- Score

40. Does privacy risk appropriately measure and monitor risk?

<--- Score

41. Are the privacy risk standards challenging?
<--- Score

42. What other areas of the group might benefit from the privacy risk team's improvements, knowledge, and learning?
<--- Score

43. Is there a recommended audit plan for routine surveillance inspections of privacy risk's gains?
<--- Score

44. Who sets the privacy risk standards?
<--- Score

45. How do you encourage people to take control and responsibility?
<--- Score

46. How do you select, collect, align, and integrate privacy risk data and information for tracking daily operations and overall organizational performance, including progress relative to strategic objectives and action plans?
<--- Score

47. Who has control over resources?
<--- Score

48. What other systems, operations, processes, and infrastructures (hiring practices, staffing, training, incentives/rewards, metrics/dashboards/scorecards, etc.) need updates, additions, changes, or deletions in order to facilitate knowledge transfer and

improvements?

<--- Score

49. How will the process owner verify improvement in present and future sigma levels, process capabilities?

<--- Score

50. What should you measure to verify efficiency gains?

<--- Score

51. Does a troubleshooting guide exist or is it needed?

<--- Score

52. Implementation Planning: is a pilot needed to test the changes before a full roll out occurs?

<--- Score

53. Do you monitor the effectiveness of your privacy risk activities?

<--- Score

54. Do you monitor the privacy risk decisions made and fine tune them as they evolve?

<--- Score

55. What are the key elements of your privacy risk performance improvement system, including your evaluation, organizational learning, and innovation processes?

<--- Score

56. How do you monitor usage and cost?

<--- Score

57. Act/Adjust: What Do you Need to Do Differently?

<--- Score

58. Is new knowledge gained imbedded in the response plan?
<--- Score

59. How might the group capture best practices and lessons learned so as to leverage improvements?
<--- Score

60. How is change control managed?
<--- Score

61. Does the response plan contain a definite closed loop continual improvement scheme (e.g., plan-do-check-act)?
<--- Score

62. Is knowledge gained on process shared and institutionalized?
<--- Score

63. Who controls critical resources?
<--- Score

64. How do controls support value?
<--- Score

65. How widespread is its use?
<--- Score

66. What do you measure to verify effectiveness gains?
<--- Score

67. Are the planned controls in place?

<--- Score

68. Who will be in control?
<--- Score

69. Who is going to spread your message?
<--- Score

70. Are the planned controls working?
<--- Score

71. What should the next improvement project be that is related to privacy risk?
<--- Score

72. Does job training on the documented procedures need to be part of the process team's education and training?
<--- Score

73. What do you stand for--and what are you against?
<--- Score

74. What adjustments to the strategies are needed?
<--- Score

75. What key inputs and outputs are being measured on an ongoing basis?
<--- Score

76. Does the privacy risk performance meet the customer's requirements?
<--- Score

77. Are documented procedures clear and easy to follow for the operators?

<--- Score

78. Is reporting being used or needed?
<--- Score

79. How will new or emerging customer needs/requirements be checked/communicated to orient the process toward meeting the new specifications and continually reducing variation?
<--- Score

80. Have new or revised work instructions resulted?
<--- Score

81. Will your goals reflect your program budget?
<--- Score

82. What is the recommended frequency of auditing?
<--- Score

83. What privacy risk standards are applicable?
<--- Score

84. How will you measure your QA plan's effectiveness?
<--- Score

85. Can you adapt and adjust to changing privacy risk situations?
<--- Score

86. Will existing staff require re-training, for example, to learn new business processes?
<--- Score

87. Are suggested corrective/restorative actions

indicated on the response plan for known causes to problems that might surface?
<--- Score

88. How do senior leaders actions reflect a commitment to the organizations privacy risk values?
<--- Score

89. Are new process steps, standards, and documentation ingrained into normal operations?
<--- Score

90. Is a response plan in place for when the input, process, or output measures indicate an 'out-of-control' condition?
<--- Score

91. What is your plan to assess your security risks?
<--- Score

92. Can support from partners be adjusted?
<--- Score

93. You may have created your quality measures at a time when you lacked resources, technology wasn't up to the required standard, or low service levels were the industry norm. Have those circumstances changed?
<--- Score

94. Will the team be available to assist members in planning investigations?
<--- Score

95. Will any special training be provided for results interpretation?

<--- Score

96. Is the privacy risk test/monitoring cost justified?
<--- Score

97. Against what alternative is success being measured?
<--- Score

98. Has identifying and assessing security and privacy risks been incorporated into the overall risk management planning?
<--- Score

Add up total points for this section:
_ _ _ _ _ = Total points for this section

Divided by: _ _ _ _ _ _ (number of statements answered) = _ _ _ _ _ _
Average score for this section

Transfer your score to the privacy risk Index at the beginning of the Self-Assessment.

CRITERION #7: SUSTAIN:

INTENT: Retain the benefits.

In my belief, the answer to this question is clearly defined:

5 Strongly Agree

4 Agree

3 Neutral

2 Disagree

1 Strongly Disagree

1. What are the top 3 things at the forefront of your privacy risk agendas for the next 3 years?
<--- Score

2. Which functions and people interact with the supplier and or customer?
<--- Score

3. What would you recommend your friend do if he/she were facing this dilemma?
<--- Score

4. How do you listen to customers to obtain actionable information?
<--- Score

5. Political -is anyone trying to undermine this project?
<--- Score

6. How do you set privacy risk stretch targets and how do you get people to not only participate in setting these stretch targets but also that they strive to achieve these?
<--- Score

7. Who will determine interim and final deadlines?
<--- Score

8. Do you have enough freaky customers in your portfolio pushing you to the limit day in and day out?
<--- Score

9. What does your signature ensure?
<--- Score

10. If you had to rebuild your organization without any traditional competitive advantages (i.e., no killer technology, promising research, innovative product/ service delivery model, etcetera), how would your people have to approach their work and collaborate together in order to create the necessary conditions for success?
<--- Score

11. What counts that you are not counting?
<--- Score

12. What privacy risk modifications can you make work for you?
<--- Score

13. How are you doing compared to your industry?
<--- Score

14. Marketing budgets are tighter, consumers are more skeptical, and social media has changed forever the way we talk about privacy risk, how do you gain traction?
<--- Score

15. Were lessons learned captured and communicated?
<--- Score

16. Who is the main stakeholder, with ultimate responsibility for driving privacy risk forward?
<--- Score

17. What will be the consequences to the stakeholder (financial, reputation etc) if privacy risk does not go ahead or fails to deliver the objectives?
<--- Score

18. What goals did you miss?
<--- Score

19. What did you miss in the interview for the worst hire you ever made?
<--- Score

20. What are you challenging?
<--- Score

21. How do you transition from the baseline to the target?
<--- Score

22. What is the purpose of privacy risk in relation to the mission?
<--- Score

23. How much contingency will be available in the budget?
<--- Score

24. What are the essentials of internal privacy risk management?
<--- Score

25. Is it economical; do you have the time and money?
<--- Score

26. Who is responsible for errors?
<--- Score

27. How can you incorporate support to ensure safe and effective use of privacy risk into the services that you provide?
<--- Score

28. Is the impact that privacy risk has shown?
<--- Score

29. What are strategies for increasing support and reducing opposition?
<--- Score

30. How do you accomplish your long range privacy

risk goals?
<--- Score

31. Is a privacy risk team work effort in place?
<--- Score

32. Are assumptions made in privacy risk stated explicitly?
<--- Score

33. What are specific privacy risk rules to follow?
<--- Score

34. Can you do all this work?
<--- Score

35. Why will customers want to buy your organizations products/services?
<--- Score

36. If you had to leave your organization for a year and the only communication you could have with employees/colleagues was a single paragraph, what would you write?
<--- Score

37. What is the recommended frequency of auditing?
<--- Score

38. Is maximizing privacy risk protection the same as minimizing privacy risk loss?
<--- Score

39. What are the key enablers to make this privacy risk move?
<--- Score

40. How do you make it meaningful in connecting privacy risk with what users do day-to-day?
<--- Score

41. Can you break it down?
<--- Score

42. How do senior leaders deploy your organizations vision and values through your leadership system, to the workforce, to key suppliers and partners, and to customers and other stakeholders, as appropriate?
<--- Score

43. If your customer were your grandmother, would you tell her to buy what you're selling?
<--- Score

44. How do you keep the momentum going?
<--- Score

45. How do you deal with privacy risk changes?
<--- Score

46. How do you ensure that implementations of privacy risk products are done in a way that ensures safety?
<--- Score

47. Where can you break convention?
<--- Score

48. What is your privacy risk strategy?
<--- Score

49. Which individuals, teams or departments will be

involved in privacy risk?
<--- Score

50. Is there any existing privacy risk governance structure?
<--- Score

51. If there were zero limitations, what would you do differently?
<--- Score

52. Do you say no to customers for no reason?
<--- Score

53. How do you stay inspired?
<--- Score

54. Who will be responsible for deciding whether privacy risk goes ahead or not after the initial investigations?
<--- Score

55. Is the privacy risk organization completing tasks effectively and efficiently?
<--- Score

56. What are the potential basics of privacy risk fraud?
<--- Score

57. How can you become more high-tech but still be high touch?
<--- Score

58. How do you engage the workforce, in addition to satisfying them?
<--- Score

59. What is the big privacy risk idea?
<--- Score

60. Who do you want your customers to become?
<--- Score

61. What is the kind of project structure that would be appropriate for your privacy risk project, should it be formal and complex, or can it be less formal and relatively simple?
<--- Score

62. If you were responsible for initiating and implementing major changes in your organization, what steps might you take to ensure acceptance of those changes?
<--- Score

63. How do you cross-sell and up-sell your privacy risk success?
<--- Score

64. How much does privacy risk help?
<--- Score

65. In the past year, what have you done (or could you have done) to increase the accurate perception of your company/brand as ethical and honest?
<--- Score

66. What are the rules and assumptions your industry operates under? What if the opposite were true?
<--- Score

67. What are the short and long-term privacy risk

goals?

<--- Score

68. How will you know that the privacy risk project has been successful?

<--- Score

69. What is effective privacy risk?

<--- Score

70. What business benefits will privacy risk goals deliver if achieved?

<--- Score

71. What must you excel at?

<--- Score

72. What would have to be true for the option on the table to be the best possible choice?

<--- Score

73. What is an unauthorized commitment?

<--- Score

74. What are the challenges?

<--- Score

75. What was the last experiment you ran?

<--- Score

76. Are you relevant? Will you be relevant five years from now? Ten?

<--- Score

77. Do you have an implicit bias for capital investments over people investments?

<--- Score

78. Will there be any necessary staff changes (redundancies or new hires)?
<--- Score

79. Operational - will it work?
<--- Score

80. What happens at your organization when people fail?
<--- Score

81. Has implementation been effective in reaching specified objectives so far?
<--- Score

82. How does privacy risk integrate with other stakeholder initiatives?
<--- Score

83. How do you foster the skills, knowledge, talents, attributes, and characteristics you want to have?
<--- Score

84. What should you stop doing?
<--- Score

85. Who will provide the final approval of privacy risk deliverables?
<--- Score

86. If no one would ever find out about your accomplishments, how would you lead differently?
<--- Score

87. What is the funding source for this project?
<--- Score

88. What projects are going on in the organization today, and what resources are those projects using from the resource pools?
<--- Score

89. How do you assess the privacy risk pitfalls that are inherent in implementing it?
<--- Score

90. How is implementation research currently incorporated into each of your goals?
<--- Score

91. Is there a work around that you can use?
<--- Score

92. How do you provide a safe environment -physically and emotionally?
<--- Score

93. What trouble can you get into?
<--- Score

94. In retrospect, of the projects that you pulled the plug on, what percent do you wish had been allowed to keep going, and what percent do you wish had ended earlier?
<--- Score

95. Who uses your product in ways you never expected?
<--- Score

96. What is your competitive advantage?
<--- Score

97. What trophy do you want on your mantle?
<--- Score

98. How long will it take to change?
<--- Score

99. Which privacy risk goals are the most important?
<--- Score

100. What is the craziest thing you can do?
<--- Score

101. Who is responsible for ensuring appropriate resources (time, people and money) are allocated to privacy risk?
<--- Score

102. What knowledge, skills and characteristics mark a good privacy risk project manager?
<--- Score

103. In a project to restructure privacy risk outcomes, which stakeholders would you involve?
<--- Score

104. Who is on the team?
<--- Score

105. What are the long-term privacy risk goals?
<--- Score

106. Are you / should you be revolutionary or evolutionary?

<--- Score

107. What are the success criteria that will indicate that privacy risk objectives have been met and the benefits delivered?
<--- Score

108. Why should you adopt a privacy risk framework?
<--- Score

109. How can you negotiate privacy risk successfully with a stubborn boss, an irate client, or a deceitful coworker?
<--- Score

110. What have been your experiences in defining long range privacy risk goals?
<--- Score

111. Who are your customers?
<--- Score

112. Are you satisfied with your current role? If not, what is missing from it?
<--- Score

113. Who will manage the integration of tools?
<--- Score

114. How will you ensure you get what you expected?
<--- Score

115. Are you changing as fast as the world around you?
<--- Score

116. What is your question? Why?
<--- Score

117. What is the overall talent health of your organization as a whole at senior levels, and for each organization reporting to a member of the Senior Leadership Team?
<--- Score

118. Are the assumptions believable and achievable?
<--- Score

119. When information truly is ubiquitous, when reach and connectivity are completely global, when computing resources are infinite, and when a whole new set of impossibilities are not only possible, but happening, what will that do to your business?
<--- Score

120. What potential megatrends could make your business model obsolete?
<--- Score

121. What is a feasible sequencing of reform initiatives over time?
<--- Score

122. Will it be accepted by users?
<--- Score

123. How do you govern and fulfill your societal responsibilities?
<--- Score

124. Do you feel that more should be done in the privacy risk area?

<--- Score

125. Is your basic point _____ or _____?
<--- Score

126. What unique value proposition (UVP) do you offer?
<--- Score

127. Why do and why don't your customers like your organization?
<--- Score

128. What have you done to protect your business from competitive encroachment?
<--- Score

129. What are your personal philosophies regarding privacy risk and how do they influence your work?
<--- Score

130. What is the range of capabilities?
<--- Score

131. What may be the consequences for the performance of an organization if all stakeholders are not consulted regarding privacy risk?
<--- Score

132. What are the barriers to increased privacy risk production?
<--- Score

133. How can you become the company that would put you out of business?
<--- Score

134. What role does communication play in the success or failure of a privacy risk project?
<--- Score

135. Are your responses positive or negative?
<--- Score

136. How do you foster innovation?
<--- Score

137. Is a privacy risk breakthrough on the horizon?
<--- Score

138. What is something you believe that nearly no one agrees with you on?
<--- Score

139. Why is privacy risk important for you now?
<--- Score

140. Do you have the right people on the bus?
<--- Score

141. What threat is privacy risk addressing?
<--- Score

142. What do we do when new problems arise?
<--- Score

143. What are the business goals privacy risk is aiming to achieve?
<--- Score

144. What you are going to do to affect the numbers?
<--- Score

145. Do you think you know, or do you know you know ?

<--- Score

146. What are your most important goals for the strategic privacy risk objectives?

<--- Score

147. Which models, tools and techniques are necessary?

<--- Score

148. How will you motivate the stakeholders with the least vested interest?

<--- Score

149. Who do you think the world wants your organization to be?

<--- Score

150. What new services of functionality will be implemented next with privacy risk ?

<--- Score

151. What are current privacy risk paradigms?

<--- Score

152. Is privacy risk realistic, or are you setting yourself up for failure?

<--- Score

153. Do you have the right capabilities and capacities?

<--- Score

154. Why not do privacy risk?

<--- Score

155. Are you using a design thinking approach and integrating Innovation, privacy risk Experience, and Brand Value?
<--- Score

156. If you do not follow, then how to lead?
<--- Score

157. Have new benefits been realized?
<--- Score

158. How do you proactively clarify deliverables and privacy risk quality expectations?
<--- Score

159. Who, on the executive team or the board, has spoken to a customer recently?
<--- Score

160. How will you insure seamless interoperability of privacy risk moving forward?
<--- Score

161. What one word do you want to own in the minds of your customers, employees, and partners?
<--- Score

162. Is there any reason to believe the opposite of my current belief?
<--- Score

163. How important is privacy risk to the user organizations mission?
<--- Score

164. To whom do you add value?
<--- Score

165. At what moment would you think; Will I get fired?
<--- Score

166. Who do we want your customers to become?
<--- Score

167. What information is critical to your organization that your executives are ignoring?
<--- Score

168. What is your formula for success in privacy risk ?
<--- Score

169. How do customers see your organization?
<--- Score

170. How do you go about securing privacy risk?
<--- Score

171. How do you determine the key elements that affect privacy risk workforce satisfaction, how are these elements determined for different workforce groups and segments?
<--- Score

172. Who are four people whose careers you have enhanced?
<--- Score

173. Have benefits been optimized with all key stakeholders?
<--- Score

174. Do you see more potential in people than they do in themselves?
<--- Score

175. How do you maintain privacy risk's Integrity?
<--- Score

176. If you weren't already in this business, would you enter it today? And if not, what are you going to do about it?
<--- Score

177. Are all key stakeholders present at all Structured Walkthroughs?
<--- Score

178. Why is it important to have senior management support for a privacy risk project?
<--- Score

179. If you find that you havent accomplished one of the goals for one of the steps of the privacy risk strategy, what will you do to fix it?
<--- Score

180. Why should people listen to you?
<--- Score

181. What is the estimated value of the project?
<--- Score

182. Instead of going to current contacts for new ideas, what if you reconnected with dormant contacts--the people you used to know? If you were going reactivate a dormant tie, who would it be?

<--- Score

183. Are you making progress, and are you making progress as privacy risk leaders?
<--- Score

184. How do you lead with privacy risk in mind?
<--- Score

185. Do you know who is a friend or a foe?
<--- Score

186. Who else should you help?
<--- Score

187. Can the schedule be done in the given time?
<--- Score

188. Do privacy risk rules make a reasonable demand on a users capabilities?
<--- Score

189. Is privacy risk dependent on the successful delivery of a current project?
<--- Score

190. Whose voice (department, ethnic group, women, older workers, etc) might you have missed hearing from in your company, and how might you amplify this voice to create positive momentum for your business?
<--- Score

191. What stupid rule would you most like to kill?
<--- Score

192. What happens if you do not have enough funding?
<--- Score

193. What are you trying to prove to yourself, and how might it be hijacking your life and business success?
<--- Score

194. Whom among your colleagues do you trust, and for what?
<--- Score

195. Are you paying enough attention to the partners your company depends on to succeed?
<--- Score

196. What are the gaps in your knowledge and experience?
<--- Score

197. Do you think privacy risk accomplishes the goals you expect it to accomplish?
<--- Score

198. What relationships among privacy risk trends do you perceive?
<--- Score

199. Are there any activities that you can take off your to do list?
<--- Score

200. Are new benefits received and understood?
<--- Score

201. How likely is it that a customer would

recommend your company to a friend or colleague?
<--- Score

202. Ask yourself: how would you do this work if you only had one staff member to do it?
<--- Score

203. How do you know if you are successful?
<--- Score

204. How do you keep records, of what?
<--- Score

205. What is the source of the strategies for privacy risk strengthening and reform?
<--- Score

206. Who are the key stakeholders?
<--- Score

207. Who is responsible for privacy risk?
<--- Score

208. What are internal and external privacy risk relations?
<--- Score

Add up total points for this section:
_ _ _ _ _ = Total points for this section

Divided by: _ _ _ _ _ _ (number of statements answered) = _ _ _ _ _ _
Average score for this section

Transfer your score to the privacy risk Index at the beginning of the Self-

Assessment.

Privacy Risk and Managing Projects, Criteria for Project Managers:

1.0 Initiating Process Group: Privacy Risk

1. Did the Privacy Risk project team have the right skills?

2. Do you understand all business (operational), technical, resource and vendor risks associated with the Privacy Risk project?

3. The Privacy Risk project you are managing has nine stakeholders. How many channel of communications are there between corresponding stakeholders?

4. What is the NEXT thing to do?

5. If the risk event occurs, what will you do?

6. What communication items need improvement?

7. Who is performing the work of the Privacy Risk project?

8. Measurable - are the targets measurable?

9. Do you know all the stakeholders impacted by the Privacy Risk project and what needs are?

10. For technology Privacy Risk projects only: Are all production support stakeholders (Business unit, technical support, & user) prepared for implementation with appropriate contingency plans?

11. What were things that you need to improve?

12. Who is funding the Privacy Risk project?

13. Does it make any difference if you am successful?

14. What input will you be required to provide the Privacy Risk project team?

15. How well did you do?

16. Do you know the Privacy Risk projects goal, purpose and objectives?

17. The process to Manage Stakeholders is part of which process group?

18. How should needs be met?

19. How do you help others satisfy needs?

20. Who does what?

1.1 Project Charter: Privacy Risk

21. Is it an improvement over existing products?

22. What barriers do you predict to your success?

23. When will this occur?

24. Name and describe the elements that deal with providing the detail?

25. What is in it for you?

26. What is the most common tool for helping define the detail?

27. How will you know a change is an improvement?

28. Why do you need to manage scope?

29. If finished, on what date did it finish?

30. What is the justification?

31. Where and how does the team fit within your organization structure?

32. Privacy Risk project deliverables: what is the Privacy Risk project going to produce?

33. What goes into your Privacy Risk project Charter?

34. Who are the stakeholders?

35. How will you know that a change is an improvement?

36. How high should you set your goals?

37. How will you learn more about the process or system you are trying to improve?

38. Who will take notes, document decisions?

39. What is the business need?

40. Why is it important?

1.2 Stakeholder Register: Privacy Risk

41. How will reports be created?

42. Who wants to talk about Security?

43. Is your organization ready for change?

44. How should employers make voices heard?

45. What & Why?

46. What is the power of the stakeholder?

47. Who is managing stakeholder engagement?

48. What are the major Privacy Risk project milestones requiring communications or providing communications opportunities?

49. What opportunities exist to provide communications?

50. How big is the gap?

51. How much influence do they have on the Privacy Risk project?

1.3 Stakeholder Analysis Matrix: Privacy Risk

52. Who is directly responsible for decisions on issues important to the Privacy Risk project?

53. Beneficiaries; who are the potential beneficiaries?

54. Processes and systems, etc?

55. How will the Privacy Risk project benefit them?

56. Which resources are required?

57. Price, value, quality?

58. Legislative effects?

59. How do you manage Privacy Risk project Risk?

60. Are you going to weigh the stakeholders?

61. Financial reserves, likely returns?

62. What advantages do your organizations stakeholders have?

63. How can you fill the need to show progress?

64. Who will be affected by the Privacy Risk project?

65. Who holds positions of responsibility in interested organizations?

66. What is the range you need to look at?

67. What are the mechanisms of public and social accountability, and how can they be made better?

68. What is your Advocacy Strategy?

69. Who is influential in the Privacy Risk project area (both thematic and geographic areas)?

70. Continuity, supply chain robustness?

71. Business and product development?

2.0 Planning Process Group: Privacy Risk

72. Is your organization showing technical capacity and leadership commitment to keep working with the Privacy Risk project and to repeat it?

73. In what ways can the governance of the Privacy Risk project be improved so that it has greater likelihood of achieving future sustainability?

74. What is the difference between the early schedule and late schedule?

75. On which process should team members spend the most time?

76. How well did the chosen processes fit the needs of the Privacy Risk project?

77. Did the program design/ implementation strategy adequately address the planning stage necessary to set up structures, hire staff etc.?

78. Is the Privacy Risk project supported by national and/or local organizations?

79. What do you need to do?

80. Professionals want to know what is expected from them; what are the deliverables?

81. To what extent has the intervention strategy been

adapted to the areas of intervention in which it is being implemented?

82. Are the necessary foundations in place to ensure the sustainability of the results of the Privacy Risk project?

83. Are the follow-up indicators relevant and do they meet the quality needed to measure the outputs and outcomes of the Privacy Risk project?

84. Privacy Risk project assessment; why did you do this Privacy Risk project?

85. If task x starts two days late, what is the effect on the Privacy Risk project end date?

86. How can you make your needs known?

87. How are it Privacy Risk projects different?

88. How does activity resource estimation affect activity duration estimation?

89. You did your readings, yes?

90. In what way has the program contributed towards the issue culture and development included on the public agenda?

91. What input will you be required to provide the Privacy Risk project team?

2.1 Project Management Plan: Privacy Risk

92. When is the Privacy Risk project management plan created?

93. How well are you able to manage your risk?

94. Do there need to be organizational changes?

95. Is the budget realistic?

96. What are the constraints?

97. Who is the Privacy Risk project Manager?

98. Is there an incremental analysis/cost effectiveness analysis of proposed mitigation features based on an approved method and using an accepted model?

99. Are there any scope changes proposed for a previously authorized Privacy Risk project?

100. Who is the sponsor?

101. Why do you manage integration?

102. What are the training needs?

103. Does the implementation plan have an appropriate division of responsibilities?

104. How do you manage time?

105. Is the appropriate plan selected based on your organizations objectives and evaluation criteria expressed in Principles and Guidelines policies?

106. Was the peer (technical) review of the cost estimates duly coordinated with the cost estimate center of expertise and addressed in the review documentation and certification?

107. What goes into your Privacy Risk project Charter?

108. What are the assigned resources?

109. How do you organize the costs in the Privacy Risk project management plan?

110. Are comparable cost estimates used for comparing, screening and selecting alternative plans, and has a reasonable cost estimate been developed for the recommended plan?

2.2 Scope Management Plan: Privacy Risk

111. Product – what are you trying to accomplish and how will you know when you are finished?

112. Are updated Privacy Risk project time & resource estimates reasonable based on the current Privacy Risk project stage?

113. Would the Privacy Risk project cost sharing involve reimbursement to the sponsor?

114. What are the risks that could significantly affect the communication on the Privacy Risk project?

115. What strengths do you have?

116. Is documentation created for communication with the suppliers and Vendors?

117. Does the quality assurance process provide objective verification of adherence to applicable standards, procedures & requirements?

118. Given the scope of the Privacy Risk project, which criterion should be optimized?

119. Have the key elements of a coherent Privacy Risk project management strategy been established?

120. Describe the manner in which Privacy Risk project deliverables will be formally presented and

accepted. Will they be presented at the end of each phase?

121. Are procurement deliverables arriving on time and to specification?

122. Are measurements and feedback mechanisms incorporated in tracking work effort & refining work estimating techniques?

123. Function of the configuration control board?

124. Organizational unit (e.g., department, team, or person) who will accept responsibility for satisfactory completion of the item?

125. Which statement about customer expectations is not true?

126. Timeline and milestones?

127. Assess the expected stability of the scope of this Privacy Risk project how likely is it to change, how frequently, and by how much?

128. Process groups – where do scope management processes fit in?

129. Is current scope of the Privacy Risk project substantially different than that originally defined?

130. What is your organizations history in doing similar activities?

2.3 Requirements Management Plan: Privacy Risk

131. Could inaccurate or incomplete requirements in this Privacy Risk project create a serious risk for the business?

132. Will the Privacy Risk project requirements become approved in writing?

133. What is a problem?

134. Do you understand the role that each stakeholder will play in the requirements process?

135. After the requirements are gathered and set forth on the requirements register, theyre little more than a laundry list of items. Some may be duplicates, some might conflict with others and some will be too broad or too vague to understand. Describe how the requirements will be analyzed. Who will perform the analysis?

136. What information regarding the Privacy Risk project requirements will be reported?

137. Do you really need to write this document at all?

138. Who will initially review the Privacy Risk project work or products to ensure it meets the applicable acceptance criteria?

139. If it exists, where is it housed?

140. Have stakeholders been instructed in the Change Control process?

141. How will you communicate scheduled tasks to other team members?

142. Who came up with this requirement?

143. How knowledgeable is the team in the proposed application area?

144. Will you use tracing to help understand the impact of a change in requirements?

145. What are you counting on?

146. How detailed should the Privacy Risk project get?

147. Are actual resource expenditures versus planned still acceptable?

148. Business analysis scope?

149. Is stakeholder risk tolerance an important factor for the requirements process in this Privacy Risk project?

150. Which hardware or software, related to, or as outcome of the Privacy Risk project is new to your organization?

2.4 Requirements Documentation: Privacy Risk

151. Completeness. are all functions required by the customer included?

152. How much testing do you need to do to prove that your system is safe?

153. Does your organization restrict technical alternatives?

154. How does what is being described meet the business need?

155. What are the acceptance criteria?

156. What images does it conjure?

157. Where are business rules being captured?

158. Does the system provide the functions which best support the customers needs?

159. Who is interacting with the system?

160. How much does requirements engineering cost?

161. What can tools do for us?

162. What variations exist for a process?

163. Do your constraints stand?

164. What if the system wasn t implemented?

165. What will be the integration problems?

166. If applicable; are there issues linked with the fact that this is an offshore Privacy Risk project?

167. Can the requirement be changed without a large impact on other requirements?

168. How do you know when a Requirement is accurate enough?

169. Where do system and software requirements come from, what are sources?

170. How to document system requirements?

2.5 Requirements Traceability Matrix: Privacy Risk

171. Why do you manage scope?

172. What percentage of Privacy Risk projects are producing traceability matrices between requirements and other work products?

173. How do you manage scope?

174. Do you have a clear understanding of all subcontracts in place?

175. Will you use a Requirements Traceability Matrix?

176. Is there a requirements traceability process in place?

177. How will it affect the stakeholders personally in career?

178. Describe the process for approving requirements so they can be added to the traceability matrix and Privacy Risk project work can be performed. Will the Privacy Risk project requirements become approved in writing?

179. What are the chronologies, contingencies, consequences, criteria?

180. How small is small enough?

181. What is the WBS?

182. Why use a WBS?

2.6 Project Scope Statement: Privacy Risk

183. Did your Privacy Risk project ask for this?

184. Is there a Change Management Board?

185. Have the configuration management functions been assigned?

186. What are the defined meeting materials?

187. What went wrong?

188. Is an issue management process documented and filed?

189. Is the quality function identified and assigned?

190. If you were to write a list of what should not be included in the scope statement, what are the things that you would recommend be described as out-of-scope?

191. If there is an independent oversight contractor, have they signed off on the Privacy Risk project Plan?

192. Are there specific processes you will use to evaluate and approve/reject changes?

193. Elements that deal with providing the detail?

194. What should you drop in order to add something

new?

195. What is a process you might recommend to verify the accuracy of the research deliverable?

196. Are there completion/verification criteria defined for each task producing an output?

197. Will statistics related to QA be collected, trends analyzed, and problems raised as issues?

198. Will the qa related information be reported regularly as part of the status reporting mechanisms?

199. Has the format for tracking and monitoring schedules and costs been defined?

200. Have you been able to thoroughly document the Privacy Risk projects assumptions and constraints?

201. Once its defined, what is the stability of the Privacy Risk project scope?

202. Privacy Risk project lead, team lead, solution architect?

2.7 Assumption and Constraint Log: Privacy Risk

203. Is this process still needed?

204. Security analysis has access to information that is sanitized?

205. Are requirements management tracking tools and procedures in place?

206. Are processes for release management of new development from coding and unit testing, to integration testing, to training, and production defined and followed?

207. Do you know what your customers expectations are regarding this process?

208. Is the steering committee active in Privacy Risk project oversight?

209. Is the definition of the Privacy Risk project scope clear; what needs to be accomplished?

210. What other teams / processes would be impacted by changes to the current process, and how?

211. Can you perform this task or activity in a more effective manner?

212. Is staff trained on the software technologies that are being used on the Privacy Risk project?

213. How do you design an auditing system?

214. Are there procedures in place to effectively manage interdependencies with other Privacy Risk projects / systems?

215. What do you audit?

216. Are there standards for code development?

217. Are there processes defining how software will be developed including development methods, overall timeline for development, software product standards, and traceability?

218. Are best practices and metrics employed to identify issues, progress, performance, etc.?

219. Contradictory information between document sections?

220. Does the traceability documentation describe the tool and/or mechanism to be used to capture traceability throughout the life cycle?

221. Model-building: what data-analytic strategies are useful when building proportional-hazards models?

2.8 Work Breakdown Structure: Privacy Risk

222. Where does it take place?

223. Is the work breakdown structure (wbs) defined and is the scope of the Privacy Risk project clear with assigned deliverable owners?

224. How big is a work-package?

225. What is the probability of completing the Privacy Risk project in less that xx days?

226. How many levels?

227. When does it have to be done?

228. When do you stop?

229. How much detail?

230. How will you and your Privacy Risk project team define the Privacy Risk projects scope and work breakdown structure?

231. What is the probability that the Privacy Risk project duration will exceed xx weeks?

232. How far down?

233. Can you make it?

234. Is it a change in scope?

235. When would you develop a Work Breakdown Structure?

236. Is it still viable?

237. Who has to do it?

238. Why would you develop a Work Breakdown Structure?

2.9 WBS Dictionary: Privacy Risk

239. Are material costs reported within the same period as that in which BCWP is earned for that material?

240. Are authorized changes being incorporated in a timely manner?

241. Is data disseminated to the contractors management timely, accurate, and usable?

242. Authorization to proceed with all authorized work?

243. Are records maintained to show how undistributed budgets are controlled?

244. Is subcontracted work defined and identified to the appropriate subcontractor within the proper WBS element?

245. Are the wbs and organizational levels for application of the Privacy Risk projected overhead costs identified?

246. Actual cost of work performed?

247. Incurrence of actual indirect costs in excess of budgets, by element of expense?

248. Does the sum of all work package budgets plus planning packages within control accounts equal the budgets assigned to the already stated control

accounts?

249. Are estimates of costs at completion generated in a rational, consistent manner?

250. Are work packages reasonably short in time duration or do they have adequate objective indicators/milestones to minimize subjectivity of the in process work evaluation?

251. Does the contractor require sufficient detailed planning of control accounts to constrain the application of budget initially allocated for future effort to current effort?

252. Appropriate work authorization documents which subdivide the contractual effort and responsibilities, within functional organizations?

253. What is the goal?

254. Knowledgeable Privacy Risk projections of future performance?

255. Are internal budgets for authorized, and not priced changes based on the contractors resource plan for accomplishing the work?

256. Does the contractors system include procedures for measuring performance of the lowest level organization responsible for the control account?

2.10 Schedule Management Plan: Privacy Risk

257. Has the business need been clearly defined?

258. Does the schedule have reasonable float?

259. Is your organization certified as a broker of the products/supplies?

260. Is there a formal set of procedures supporting Stakeholder Management?

261. Does the detailed work plan match the complexity of tasks with the capabilities of personnel?

262. Have Privacy Risk project management standards and procedures been identified / established and documented?

263. Have key stakeholders been identified?

264. Are there checklists created to determine if all quality processes are followed?

265. Have activity relationships and interdependencies within tasks been adequately identified?

266. Is there a Steering Committee in place?

267. Does the Privacy Risk project have a formal Privacy Risk project Charter?

268. Have all necessary approvals been obtained?

269. Are mitigation strategies identified?

270. Can be realistically shortened (the duration of subsequent tasks)?

271. Are non-critical path items updated and agreed upon with the teams?

272. Is stakeholder involvement adequate?

273. Who is responsible for estimating the activity resources?

274. Are the results of quality assurance reviews provided to affected groups & individuals?

275. How relevant is this attribute to this Privacy Risk project or audit?

276. Were Privacy Risk project team members involved in the development of activity & task decomposition?

2.11 Activity List: Privacy Risk

277. What is the probability the Privacy Risk project can be completed in xx weeks?

278. What is the total time required to complete the Privacy Risk project if no delays occur?

279. How will it be performed?

280. Is infrastructure setup part of your Privacy Risk project?

281. What went well?

282. What did not go as well?

283. The wbs is developed as part of a joint planning session. and how do you know that youhave done this right?

284. For other activities, how much delay can be tolerated?

285. How can the Privacy Risk project be displayed graphically to better visualize the activities?

286. Can you determine the activity that must finish, before this activity can start?

287. How should ongoing costs be monitored to try to keep the Privacy Risk project within budget?

288. How difficult will it be to do specific activities on

this Privacy Risk project?

289. When do the individual activities need to start and finish?

290. What went right?

291. Should you include sub-activities?

292. How do you determine the late start (LS) for each activity?

293. What will be performed?

294. Where will it be performed?

295. What is the LF and LS for each activity?

2.12 Activity Attributes: Privacy Risk

296. Were there other ways you could have organized the data to achieve similar results?

297. Does your organization of the data change its meaning?

298. Time for overtime?

299. What is missing?

300. Resources to accomplish the work?

301. Are the required resources available?

302. Can you re-assign any activities to another resource to resolve an over-allocation?

303. Activity: what is In the Bag?

304. Are the required resources available or need to be acquired?

305. Have constraints been applied to the start and finish milestones for the phases?

306. Activity: what is Missing?

307. What activity do you think you should spend the most time on?

308. How much activity detail is required?

309. How many resources do you need to complete the work scope within a limit of X number of days?

310. How difficult will it be to do specific activities on this Privacy Risk project?

311. Has management defined a definite timeframe for the turnaround or Privacy Risk project window?

312. Have you identified the Activity Leveling Priority code value on each activity?

313. What is the general pattern here?

2.13 Milestone List: Privacy Risk

314. Milestone pages should display the UserID of the person who added the milestone. Does a report or query exist that provides this audit information?

315. How soon can the activity finish?

316. Which path is the critical path?

317. How will the milestone be verified?

318. Obstacles faced?

319. Describe your organizations strengths and core competencies. What factors will make your organization succeed?

320. Effects on core activities, distraction?

321. How difficult will it be to do specific activities on this Privacy Risk project?

322. When will the Privacy Risk project be complete?

323. Gaps in capabilities?

324. What is the market for your technology, product or service?

325. Marketing - reach, distribution, awareness?

326. Environmental effects?

327. What has been done so far?

328. Level of the Innovation?

329. Global influences?

330. How late can the activity finish?

2.14 Network Diagram: Privacy Risk

331. If a current contract exists, can you provide the vendor name, contract start, and contract expiration date?

332. What activity must be completed immediately before this activity can start?

333. What are the Key Success Factors?

334. Review the logical flow of the network diagram. Take a look at which activities you have first and then sequence the activities. Do they make sense?

335. Planning: who, how long, what to do?

336. What job or jobs follow it?

337. Why must you schedule milestones, such as reviews, throughout the Privacy Risk project?

338. What activities must follow this activity?

339. What is the completion time?

340. What is the lowest cost to complete this Privacy Risk project in xx weeks?

341. Where do schedules come from?

342. Are you on time?

343. What are the tools?

344. If the Privacy Risk project network diagram cannot change and you have extra personnel resources, what is the BEST thing to do?

345. What job or jobs could run concurrently?

346. Where do you schedule uncertainty time?

347. What can be done concurrently?

348. What is the probability of completing the Privacy Risk project in less that xx days?

349. What activities must occur simultaneously with this activity?

2.15 Activity Resource Requirements: Privacy Risk

350. How many signatures do you require on a check and does this match what is in your policy and procedures?

351. Do you use tools like decomposition and rolling-wave planning to produce the activity list and other outputs?

352. Why do you do that?

353. Which logical relationship does the PDM use most often?

354. Anything else?

355. When does monitoring begin?

356. Organizational Applicability?

357. Is there anything planned that does not need to be here?

358. Are there unresolved issues that need to be addressed?

359. How do you handle petty cash?

360. What is the Work Plan Standard?

361. What are constraints that you might find during

the Human Resource Planning process?

362. Other support in specific areas?

2.16 Resource Breakdown Structure: Privacy Risk

363. How difficult will it be to do specific activities on this Privacy Risk project?

364. How can this help you with team building?

365. Which resources should be in the resource pool?

366. Why do you do it?

367. Who needs what information?

368. What is the purpose of assigning and documenting responsibility?

369. Is predictive resource analysis being done?

370. What is the difference between % Complete and % work?

371. Who will use the system?

372. Any changes from stakeholders?

373. Who will be used as a Privacy Risk project team member?

374. What is the primary purpose of the human resource plan?

375. When do they need the information?

2.17 Activity Duration Estimates: Privacy Risk

376. Would you rate yourself as being risk-averse, risk-neutral, or risk-seeking?

377. Does a process exist for approving or rejecting changes?

378. Find an example of a contract for information technology services. Analyze the key features of the contract. What type of contract was used and why?

379. List five reasons why organizations outsource. Why is there a growing trend in outsourcing, especially in the government?

380. After how many days will the lease cost be the same as the purchase cost for the equipment?

381. Is a formal written notice that the contract is complete provided to the seller?

382. What do corresponding sources say about Privacy Risk project management?

383. Is a contract developed which obligates the seller and the buyer?

384. How can you use Microsoft Privacy Risk project and Excel to assist in Privacy Risk project risk management?

385. Is corrective action taken to bring Privacy Risk project performance into line with the Privacy Risk project plan?

386. What are two suggestions for ensuring adequate change control on Privacy Risk projects that involve outside contracts?

387. Will it help promote wellness at your organization and reduce insurance costs?

388. Do you agree with the suggestions provided for improving Privacy Risk project communications?

389. Does a process exist to identify which qualified resources may be attainable?

390. How have experts such as Deming, Juran, Crosby, and Taguchi affected the quality movement and todays use of Six Sigma?

391. Consider the changes in the job market for information technology workers. How does the job market and current state of the economy affect human resource management?

392. Why do you need a good WBS to use Privacy Risk project management software?

2.18 Duration Estimating Worksheet: Privacy Risk

393. What is next?

394. Is the Privacy Risk project responsive to community need?

395. What are the critical bottleneck activities?

396. When does your organization expect to be able to complete it?

397. What is the total time required to complete the Privacy Risk project if no delays occur?

398. Value pocket identification & quantification what are value pockets?

399. How should ongoing costs be monitored to try to keep the Privacy Risk project within budget?

400. Do any colleagues have experience with your organization and/or RFPs?

401. What info is needed?

402. When, then?

403. What is cost and Privacy Risk project cost management?

404. Define the work as completely as possible. What

work will be included in the Privacy Risk project?

405. Done before proceeding with this activity or what can be done concurrently?

406. What utility impacts are there?

407. Will the Privacy Risk project collaborate with the local community and leverage resources?

408. Science = process: remember the scientific method?

2.19 Project Schedule: Privacy Risk

409. If you can not fix it, how do you do it differently?

410. Your best shot for providing estimations how complex/how much work does the activity require?

411. How closely did the initial Privacy Risk project Schedule compare with the actual schedule?

412. Is Privacy Risk project work proceeding in accordance with the original Privacy Risk project schedule?

413. Are there activities that came from a template or previous Privacy Risk project that are not applicable on this phase of this Privacy Risk project?

414. How detailed should a Privacy Risk project get?

415. Why is software Privacy Risk project disaster so common?

416. What is the difference?

417. What is the purpose of a Privacy Risk project schedule?

418. Why do you think schedule issues often cause the most conflicts on Privacy Risk projects?

419. How much slack is available in the Privacy Risk project?

420. Are the original Privacy Risk project schedule and budget realistic?

421. Did the Privacy Risk project come in under budget?

422. Are activities connected because logic dictates the order in which others occur?

423. What does that mean?

424. Privacy Risk project work estimates Who is managing the work estimate quality of work tasks in the Privacy Risk project schedule?

425. Does the condition or event threaten the Privacy Risk projects objectives in any ways?

426. Are procedures defined by which the Privacy Risk project schedule may be changed?

2.20 Cost Management Plan: Privacy Risk

427. How relevant is this attribute to this Privacy Risk project or audit?

428. Has the scope management document been updated and distributed to help prevent scope creep?

429. Do all stakeholders know how to access this repository and where to find the Privacy Risk project documentation?

430. Is a payment system in place with proper reviews and approvals?

431. Have stakeholder accountabilities & responsibilities been clearly defined?

432. Cost management – how will the cost of changes be estimated and controlled?

433. Are the quality tools and methods identified in the Quality Plan appropriate to the Privacy Risk project?

434. Are target dates established for each milestone deliverable?

435. Privacy Risk project definition & scope?

436. Change types and category – What are the types of changes and what are the techniques to report and

control changes?

437. Who should write the PEP?

438. Have Privacy Risk project team accountabilities & responsibilities been clearly defined?

439. Vac -variance at completion, how much over/ under budget do you expect to be?

440. If you sold 10x widgets on a day, what would the affect on costs be?

441. Exclusions – is there scope to be performed or provided by others?

442. Are schedule deliverables actually delivered?

443. Forecasts – how will the cost to complete the Privacy Risk project be forecast?

444. What would you do differently what did not work?

2.21 Activity Cost Estimates: Privacy Risk

445. How do you change activities?

446. Eac -estimate at completion, what is the total job expected to cost?

447. How do you do activity recasts?

448. Did the consultant work with local staff to develop local capacity?

449. Which contract type places the most risk on the seller?

450. Padding is bad and contingencies are good. what is the difference?

451. Was the consultant knowledgeable about the program?

452. How do you allocate indirect costs to activities?

453. What areas were overlooked on this Privacy Risk project?

454. What makes a good activity description?

455. In which phase of the acquisition process cycle does source qualifications reside?

456. Will you need to provide essential services

information about activities?

457. Is there anything unique in this Privacy Risk projects scope statement that will affect resources?

458. Who determines the quality and expertise of contractors?

459. What is the activity inventory?

460. How do you fund change orders?

461. Is costing method consistent with study goals?

462. How many activities should you have?

2.22 Cost Estimating Worksheet: Privacy Risk

463. What is the estimated labor cost today based upon this information?

464. Is the Privacy Risk project responsive to community need?

465. Will the Privacy Risk project collaborate with the local community and leverage resources?

466. What happens to any remaining funds not used?

467. Who is best positioned to know and assist in identifying corresponding factors?

468. Is it feasible to establish a control group arrangement?

469. Ask: are others positioned to know, are others credible, and will others cooperate?

470. Identify the timeframe necessary to monitor progress and collect data to determine how the selected measure has changed?

471. Does the Privacy Risk project provide innovative ways for stakeholders to overcome obstacles or deliver better outcomes?

472. What is the purpose of estimating?

473. What additional Privacy Risk project(s) could be initiated as a result of this Privacy Risk project?

474. What costs are to be estimated?

475. What will others want?

476. Can a trend be established from historical performance data on the selected measure and are the criteria for using trend analysis or forecasting methods met?

477. What can be included?

478. How will the results be shared and to whom?

2.23 Cost Baseline: Privacy Risk

479. Have the lessons learned been filed with the Privacy Risk project Management Office?

480. What weaknesses do you have?

481. If you sold 10x widgets on a day, what would the affect on profits be?

482. Has the actual cost of the Privacy Risk project (or Privacy Risk project phase) been tallied and compared to the approved budget?

483. Escalation criteria met?

484. Are procedures defined by which the cost baseline may be changed?

485. What is the reality?

486. Impact to environment?

487. Have all approved changes to the schedule baseline been identified and impact on the Privacy Risk project documented?

488. Are you meeting with your team regularly?

489. Has the documentation relating to operation and maintenance of the product(s) or service(s) been delivered to, and accepted by, operations management?

490. Has the Privacy Risk project documentation been archived or otherwise disposed as described in the Privacy Risk project communication plan?

491. Have all approved changes to the cost baseline been identified and impact on the Privacy Risk project documented?

492. What deliverables come first?

493. Is there anything you need from upper management in order to be successful?

494. Pcs for your new business. what would the life cycle costs be?

495. Are you asking management for something as a result of this update?

496. For what purpose ?

497. Is the cr within Privacy Risk project scope?

498. What is it ?

2.24 Quality Management Plan: Privacy Risk

499. How do senior leaders create an environment that encourages learning and innovation?

500. Does a prospective decision remain the same regardless of what the data show is?

501. What are your results for key measures/indicators of accomplishment of organizational strategy?

502. List your organizations customer contact standards that employees are expected to maintain. How are corresponding standards measured?

503. What does it do for you (or to me)?

504. Are there procedures in place to effectively manage interdependencies with other Privacy Risk projects / systems?

505. Checking the completeness and appropriateness of the sampling and testing. Were the right locations/ samples tested for the right parameters?

506. Have Privacy Risk project management standards and procedures been established and documented?

507. What is quality and how will you ensure it?

508. How do you ensure that your sampling methods and procedures meet your data needs?

509. How do you decide who is responsible for signing the data reports?

510. What is the Difference Between a QMP and QAPP?

511. Do trained quality assurance auditors conduct the audits as defined in the Quality Management Plan and scheduled by the Privacy Risk project manager?

512. Is the amount of effort justified by the anticipated value of forming a new process?

513. How does your organization determine the requirements and product/service features important to customers?

514. Have adequate resources been provided by management to ensure Privacy Risk project success?

515. How is the information recorded?

516. What methods are used?

517. Is it necessary?

518. Diagrams and tables to account for complex concepts and increase overall readability?

2.25 Quality Metrics: Privacy Risk

519. How should customers provide input?

520. Were quality attributes reported?

521. Is material complete (and does it meet the standards)?

522. Was material distributed on time?

523. How can the effectiveness of each of the activities be measured?

524. What is the timeline to meet your goal?

525. Is there a set of procedures to capture, analyze and act on quality metrics?

526. What is the benchmark?

527. What metrics are important and most beneficial to measure?

528. How are requirements conflicts resolved?

529. Are there any open risk issues?

530. When is the security analysis testing complete?

531. Were number of defects identified?

532. Who notifies stakeholders of normal and abnormal results?

533. Have risk areas been identified?

534. Which are the right metrics to use?

535. Are quality metrics defined?

536. What happens if you get an abnormal result?

537. Is quality culture a competitive advantage?

2.26 Process Improvement Plan: Privacy Risk

538. What actions are needed to address the problems and achieve the goals?

539. Does your process ensure quality?

540. Does explicit definition of the measures exist?

541. Why do you want to achieve the goal?

542. Everyone agrees on what process improvement is, right?

543. Are you making progress on the goals?

544. Where do you want to be?

545. Have the frequency of collection and the points in the process where measurements will be made been determined?

546. To elicit goal statements, do you ask a question such as, What do you want to achieve?

547. If a process improvement framework is being used, which elements will help the problems and goals listed?

548. Has a process guide to collect the data been developed?

549. Who should prepare the process improvement action plan?

550. What lessons have you learned so far?

551. What personnel are the coaches for your initiative?

552. Has the time line required to move measurement results from the points of collection to databases or users been established?

553. Modeling current processes is great, and will you ever see a return on that investment?

554. What personnel are the champions for the initiative?

555. Have the supporting tools been developed or acquired?

2.27 Responsibility Assignment Matrix: Privacy Risk

556. What do people write/say on status/Privacy Risk project reports?

557. Do you know how your people are allocated?

558. Undistributed budgets, if any?

559. Are management actions taken to reduce indirect costs when there are significant adverse variances?

560. Contemplated overhead expenditure for each period based on the best information currently available?

561. Does the contractors system include procedures for measuring the performance of critical subcontractors?

562. Changes in the overhead pool and/or organization structures?

563. Are people afraid to let you know when others are under allocated?

564. Who is responsible for work and budgets for each wbs?

565. With too many people labeled as doing the work, are there too many hands involved?

566. How do you assist them to be as productive as possible?

567. What materials and procurements needed?

568. Are overhead cost budgets established for each organization which has authority to incur overhead costs?

569. Time-phased control account budgets?

570. Competencies and craftsmanship – what competencies are necessary and what level?

571. Who is going to do that work?

572. Does each role with Accountable responsibility have the authority within your organization to make the required decisions?

573. Does the contractor use objective results, design reviews, and tests to trace schedule?

574. Contract line items and end items?

2.28 Roles and Responsibilities: Privacy Risk

575. Is feedback clearly communicated and non-judgmental?

576. Accountabilities: what are the roles and responsibilities of individual team members?

577. Key conclusions and recommendations: Are conclusions and recommendations relevant and acceptable?

578. What should you do now to prepare yourself for a promotion, increased responsibilities or a different job?

579. Was the expectation clearly communicated?

580. Be specific; avoid generalities. Thank you and great work alone are insufficient. What exactly do you appreciate and why?

581. Do you take the time to clearly define roles and responsibilities on Privacy Risk project tasks?

582. Are your policies supportive of a culture of quality data?

583. What specific behaviors did you observe?

584. What is working well?

585. Are governance roles and responsibilities documented?

586. Is there a training program in place for stakeholders covering expectations, roles and responsibilities and any addition knowledge others need to be good stakeholders?

587. What areas would you highlight for changes or improvements?

588. Once the responsibilities are defined for the Privacy Risk project, have the deliverables, roles and responsibilities been clearly communicated to every participant?

589. What should you do now to prepare for your career 5+ years from now?

590. Are Privacy Risk project team roles and responsibilities identified and documented?

591. How well did the Privacy Risk project Team understand the expectations of specific roles and responsibilities?

592. What should you highlight for improvement?

593. Is the data complete?

594. What should you do now to ensure that you are exceeding expectations and excelling in your current position?

2.29 Human Resource Management Plan: Privacy Risk

595. Are action items captured and managed?

596. How complete is the human resource management plan?

597. What talent is needed?

598. What were things that you did well, and could improve, and how?

599. Are key risk mitigation strategies added to the Privacy Risk project schedule?

600. How are you going to ensure that you have a well motivated workforce?

601. Does the schedule include Privacy Risk project management time and change request analysis time?

602. Are people motivated to meet the current and future challenges?

603. Are Privacy Risk project team roles and responsibilities identified and documented?

604. Is this Privacy Risk project carried out in partnership with other groups/organizations?

605. Who will be impacted (both positively and negatively) as a result of or during the execution of

this Privacy Risk project?

606. Have reserves been created to address risks?

607. Is there a set of procedures defining the scope, procedures, and deliverables defining quality control?

608. Are meeting minutes captured and sent out after the meeting?

609. Are all resource assumptions documented?

610. Is there a Quality Management Plan?

611. Has a sponsor been identified?

612. Who is evaluated?

2.30 Communications Management Plan: Privacy Risk

613. Who have you worked with in past, similar initiatives?

614. Will messages be directly related to the release strategy or phases of the Privacy Risk project?

615. Who to share with?

616. What steps can you take for a positive relationship?

617. Who did you turn to if you had questions?

618. Where do team members get information?

619. What approaches do you use?

620. Is there an important stakeholder who is actively opposed and will not receive messages?

621. What is the stakeholders level of authority?

622. Why do you manage communications?

623. Are there common objectives between the team and the stakeholder?

624. Who is responsible?

625. Do you feel more overwhelmed by stakeholders?

626. Who needs to know and how much?

627. Are stakeholders internal or external?

628. Why is stakeholder engagement important?

629. What is the political influence?

630. Which team member will work with each stakeholder?

631. Who will use or be affected by the result of a Privacy Risk project?

632. Conflict resolution -which method when?

2.31 Risk Management Plan: Privacy Risk

633. How would you suggest monitoring for risk transition indicators?

634. Do you have a consistent repeatable process that is actually used?

635. Was an original risk assessment/risk management plan completed?

636. Are the best people available?

637. Are the metrics meaningful and useful?

638. What should be done with non-critical risks?

639. Are there new risks that mitigation strategies might introduce?

640. Are people attending meetings and doing work?

641. Maximize short-term return on investment?

642. Prioritized components/features?

643. Mitigation -how can you avoid the risk?

644. How is risk identification performed?

645. How risk averse are you?

646. Do requirements put excessive performance constraints on the product?

647. What can you do to minimize the impact if it does?

648. Who should be notified of the occurrence of each of the indicators?

649. Market risk: will the new product be useful to your organization or marketable to others?

650. Number of users of the product?

651. What did not work so well?

2.32 Risk Register: Privacy Risk

652. Are corrective measures implemented as planned?

653. What is a Risk?

654. What is the reason for current performance gaps and do the risks and opportunities identified previously account for this?

655. Risk categories: what are the main categories of risks that should be addressed on this Privacy Risk project?

656. What are the main aims, objectives of the policy, strategy, or service and the intended outcomes?

657. Risk probability and impact: how will the probabilities and impacts of risk items be assessed?

658. What are the assumptions and current status that support the assessment of the risk?

659. What are the major risks facing the Privacy Risk project?

660. Have other controls and solutions been implemented in other services which could be applied as an alternative to additional funding?

661. How well are risks controlled?

662. Methodology: how will risk management be

performed on this Privacy Risk project?

663. What evidence do you have to justify the likelihood score of the risk (audit, incident report, claim, complaints, inspection, internal review)?

664. Are implemented controls working as others should?

665. Who is going to do it?

666. When is it going to be done?

667. What will be done?

668. How is a Community Risk Register created?

669. Does the evidence highlight any areas to advance opportunities or foster good relations. If yes what steps will be taken?

670. What can be done about it?

2.33 Probability and Impact Assessment: Privacy Risk

671. Who should be notified of the occurrence of each of the risk indicators?

672. Risk categorization -which of your categories has more risk than others?

673. What new technologies are being explored in the same area?

674. What action do you usually take against risks?

675. What is the probability of the risk occurring?

676. Is the customer willing to participate in reviews?

677. How solid is the Privacy Risk projection of competitive reaction?

678. Is there additional information that would make you more confident about your analysis?

679. How would you assess the risk management process in the Privacy Risk project?

680. Is the customer willing to commit significant time to the requirements gathering process?

681. Do the requirements require the creation of new algorithms?

682. How will economic events and trends likely affect the Privacy Risk project?

683. Do requirements demand the use of new analysis, design, or testing methods?

684. What are the uncertainties associated with the technology selected for the Privacy Risk project?

685. Risk data quality assessment - what is the quality of the data used to determine or assess the risk?

686. Are the risk data complete?

687. Costs associated with late delivery or a defective product?

688. What significant shift will occur in governmental policies, laws, and regulations pertaining to specific industries?

689. Risk urgency assessment -which of your risks could occur soon, or require a longer planning time?

690. Are the risk data timely and relevant?

2.34 Probability and Impact Matrix: Privacy Risk

691. What can you do about it?

692. Lay ground work for future returns?

693. While preparing your risk responses, you identify additional risks. What should you do?

694. Workarounds are determined during which step of risk management?

695. Are staff committed for the duration of the Privacy Risk project?

696. What are its business ethics?

697. How will the consumption pattern change?

698. What is the level of commitment and professionalism?

699. What are the current or emerging trends of culture?

700. How do you manage Privacy Risk project Risk?

701. Economic to take on the Privacy Risk project?

702. Who are the owners?

703. How solid is the Privacy Risk projection of

competitive reaction?

704. What is your anticipated volatility of the requirements?

705. What will be the likely incidence of conflict with neighboring Privacy Risk projects?

706. What is the impact if the risk does occur?

707. How completely has the customer been identified?

708. Several experts are offsite, and wish to be included. How can this be done?

709. What lifestyle shifts might occur in society?

2.35 Risk Data Sheet: Privacy Risk

710. What are you here for (Mission)?

711. What was measured?

712. What are you trying to achieve (Objectives)?

713. What do you know?

714. What are your core values?

715. What are you weak at and therefore need to do better?

716. Whom do you serve (customers)?

717. What is the environment within which you operate (social trends, economic, community values, broad based participation, national directions etc.)?

718. What will be the consequences if the risk happens?

719. How reliable is the data source?

720. Who has a vested interest in how you perform as your organization (our stakeholders)?

721. What do people affected think about the need for, and practicality of preventive measures?

722. What are the main threats to your existence?

723. Risk of what?

724. What actions can be taken to eliminate or remove risk?

725. What are the main opportunities available to you that you should grab while you can?

726. What can you do?

727. What can happen?

2.36 Procurement Management Plan: Privacy Risk

728. Is there an on-going process in place to monitor Privacy Risk project risks?

729. Is the communication plan being followed?

730. Published materials?

731. Does the Privacy Risk project have a Quality Culture?

732. Are vendor invoices audited for accuracy before payment?

733. How will multiple providers be managed?

734. Financial capacity; does the seller have, or can the seller reasonably be expected to obtain, the financial resources needed?

735. Are changes in deliverable commitments agreed to by all affected groups & individuals?

736. Is Privacy Risk project work proceeding in accordance with the original Privacy Risk project schedule?

737. Is the quality assurance team identified?

738. Are the quality tools and methods identified in the Quality Plan appropriate to the Privacy Risk

project?

739. Do all stakeholders know how to access the PM repository and where to find the Privacy Risk project documentation?

740. Why is procurement planning important?

741. Are meeting minutes captured and sent out after meetings?

742. Are any non-compliance issues that exist communicated to your organization?

743. Are enough systems & user personnel assigned to the Privacy Risk project?

744. Do Privacy Risk project teams & team members report on status / activities / progress?

745. What are your quality assurance overheads?

2.37 Source Selection Criteria: Privacy Risk

746. What should be considered?

747. When is it appropriate to issue a Draft Request for Proposal (DRFP)?

748. When must you conduct a debriefing?

749. Are they compliant with all technical requirements?

750. How much past performance information should be requested?

751. Are responses to considerations adequate?

752. How will you evaluate offerors proposals?

753. How should comments received in response to a RFP be handled?

754. What information is to be provided and when should it be provided?

755. How important is cost in the source selection decision relative to past performance and technical considerations?

756. Is a cost realism analysis used?

757. How and when do you enter into Privacy Risk

project Procurement Management?

758. In order of importance, which evaluation criteria are the most critical to the determination of your overall rating?

759. What past performance information should be requested?

760. What documentation should be used to support the selection decision?

761. Is the contracting office likely to receive more purchase requests for this item or service during the coming year?

762. How do you ensure an integrated assessment of proposals?

763. How do you manage procurement?

764. What should preproposal conferences accomplish?

2.38 Stakeholder Management Plan: Privacy Risk

765. Are Privacy Risk project leaders committed to this Privacy Risk project full time?

766. Were the budget estimates reasonable?

767. Are decisions captured in a decisions log?

768. Are the Privacy Risk project team members located locally to the users/stakeholders?

769. Have the procedures for identifying budget variances been followed?

770. Are written status reports provided on a designated frequent basis?

771. Are communication systems proposed compatible with staff skills and experience?

772. Are there checklists created to demine if all quality processes are followed?

773. Is Privacy Risk project status reviewed with the steering and executive teams at appropriate intervals?

774. Does the Privacy Risk project have a formal Privacy Risk project Charter?

775. Has a structured approach been used to break work effort into manageable components (WBS)?

776. Are there any potential occupational health and safety issues due to the proposed purchases?

777. Has a quality assurance plan been developed for the Privacy Risk project?

778. Do Privacy Risk project managers participating in the Privacy Risk project know the Privacy Risk projects true status first hand?

779. Are regulatory inspections considered part of quality control?

780. Will Privacy Risk project success require up to date information at a moments notice?

2.39 Change Management Plan: Privacy Risk

781. Why would a Privacy Risk project run more smoothly when change management is emphasized from the beginning?

782. Have the systems been configured and tested?

783. Who might be able to help you the most?

784. What type of materials/channels will be available to leverage?

785. What prerequisite knowledge do corresponding groups need?

786. Has the training co-ordinator been provided with the training details and put in place the necessary arrangements?

787. What are the specific target groups/audiences that will be impacted by this change?

788. What do you expect the target audience to do, say, think or feel as a result of this communication?

789. Different application of an existing process?

790. How will you deal with anger about the restricting of communications due to confidentiality considerations?

791. How much change management is needed?

792. Has a training need analysis been carried out?

793. Do you need a new organization structure?

794. What skills, education, knowledge, or work experiences should the resources have for each identified competency?

795. How might they respond to the message and if the response may be negative or open to misinterpretation, what else needs to be said?

796. Who might present the most resistance?

797. What are you trying to achieve as a result of communication?

798. Where will the funds come from?

799. How do you gain sponsors buy-in to the communication plan?

800. Who will do the training?

3.0 Executing Process Group: Privacy Risk

801. What are the main parts of the scope statement?

802. Will a new application be developed using existing hardware, software, and networks?

803. What are the Privacy Risk project management deliverables of each process group?

804. Do the partners have sufficient financial capacity to keep up the benefits produced by the programme?

805. How can software assist in Privacy Risk project communications?

806. Is the Privacy Risk project making progress in helping to achieve the set results?

807. How can software assist in procuring goods and services?

808. What are the key components of the Privacy Risk project communications plan?

809. Have operating capacities been created and/or reinforced in partners?

810. How well defined and documented were the Privacy Risk project management processes you chose to use?

811. What is the product of your Privacy Risk project?

812. Do the products created live up to the necessary quality?

813. What are the challenges Privacy Risk project teams face?

814. What does it mean to take a systems view of a Privacy Risk project?

815. What is the difference between using brainstorming and the Delphi technique for risk identification?

816. If a risk event occurs, what will you do?

817. Does the Privacy Risk project team have enough people to execute the Privacy Risk project plan?

818. How can your organization use a weighted decision matrix to evaluate proposals as part of source selection?

819. Do Privacy Risk project managers understand your organizational context for Privacy Risk projects?

820. Are escalated issues resolved promptly?

3.1 Team Member Status Report: Privacy Risk

821. Are your organizations Privacy Risk projects more successful over time?

822. How much risk is involved?

823. How it is to be done?

824. Why is it to be done?

825. What specific interest groups do you have in place?

826. Does your organization have the means (staff, money, contract, etc.) to produce or to acquire the product, good, or service?

827. How will resource planning be done?

828. Are the products of your organizations Privacy Risk projects meeting customers objectives?

829. How can you make it practical?

830. Does the product, good, or service already exist within your organization?

831. Is there evidence that staff is taking a more professional approach toward management of your organizations Privacy Risk projects?

832. What is to be done?

833. Are the attitudes of staff regarding Privacy Risk project work improving?

834. When a teams productivity and success depend on collaboration and the efficient flow of information, what generally fails them?

835. Do you have an Enterprise Privacy Risk project Management Office (EPMO)?

836. Will the staff do training or is that done by a third party?

837. Does every department have to have a Privacy Risk project Manager on staff?

838. The problem with Reward & Recognition Programs is that the truly deserving people all too often get left out. How can you make it practical?

839. How does this product, good, or service meet the needs of the Privacy Risk project and your organization as a whole?

3.2 Change Request: Privacy Risk

840. What can be filed?

841. Should staff call into the helpdesk or go to the website?

842. How do you get changes (code) out in a timely manner?

843. Since there are no change requests in your Privacy Risk project at this point, what must you have before you begin?

844. What is the relationship between requirements attributes and reliability?

845. Are change requests logged and managed?

846. Who needs to approve change requests?

847. How can you ensure that changes have been made properly?

848. Will this change conflict with other requirements changes (e.g., lead to conflicting operational scenarios)?

849. What is the purpose of change control?

850. Where do changes come from?

851. Should a more thorough impact analysis be conducted?

852. What kind of information about the change request needs to be captured?

853. What are the duties of the change control team?

854. How does a team identify the discrete elements of a configuration?

855. How to get changes (code) out in a timely manner?

856. Have scm procedures for noting the change, recording it, and reporting it been followed?

857. Is it feasible to use requirements attributes as predictors of reliability?

858. What are the basic mechanics of the Change Advisory Board (CAB)?

3.3 Change Log: Privacy Risk

859. Does the suggested change request represent a desired enhancement to the products functionality?

860. When was the request submitted?

861. When was the request approved?

862. How does this change affect scope?

863. Is the requested change request a result of changes in other Privacy Risk project(s)?

864. Is the change request within Privacy Risk project scope?

865. Who initiated the change request?

866. Does the suggested change request seem to represent a necessary enhancement to the product?

867. Is this a mandatory replacement?

868. Is the change backward compatible without limitations?

869. Is the change request open, closed or pending?

870. How does this relate to the standards developed for specific business processes?

871. Do the described changes impact on the integrity or security of the system?

872. Is the submitted change a new change or a modification of a previously approved change?

873. Will the Privacy Risk project fail if the change request is not executed?

874. How does this change affect the timeline of the schedule?

3.4 Decision Log: Privacy Risk

875. Who is the decisionmaker?

876. What is the line where eDiscovery ends and document review begins?

877. What makes you different or better than others companies selling the same thing?

878. How does the use a Decision Support System influence the strategies/tactics or costs?

879. Is everything working as expected?

880. What are the cost implications?

881. Behaviors; what are guidelines that the team has identified that will assist them with getting the most out of team meetings?

882. How does an increasing emphasis on cost containment influence the strategies and tactics used?

883. Adversarial environment. is your opponent open to a non-traditional workflow, or will it likely challenge anything you do?

884. With whom was the decision shared or considered?

885. Does anything need to be adjusted?

886. It becomes critical to track and periodically revisit both operational effectiveness; Are you noticing all that you need to, and are you interpreting what you see effectively?

887. Which variables make a critical difference?

888. How does provision of information, both in terms of content and presentation, influence acceptance of alternative strategies?

889. What is the average size of your matters in an applicable measurement?

890. What is your overall strategy for quality control / quality assurance procedures?

891. How consolidated and comprehensive a story can you tell by capturing currently available incident data in a central location and through a log of key decisions during an incident?

892. Meeting purpose; why does this team meet?

893. Who will be given a copy of this document and where will it be kept?

894. What was the rationale for the decision?

3.5 Quality Audit: Privacy Risk

895. Health and safety arrangements; stress management workshops. How does your organization know that it provides a safe and healthy environment?

896. Is the reports overall tone appropriate?

897. How does your organization know that its system for recruiting the best staff possible are appropriately effective and constructive?

898. Are all records associated with the reconditioning of a device maintained for a minimum of two years after the sale or disposal of the last device within a lot of merchandise?

899. Are multiple statements on the same issue consistent with each other?

900. How does your organization know that its system for commercializing research outputs is appropriately effective and constructive?

901. Will the evidence likely be sufficient and appropriate?

902. Are salvageable and salvaged medical devices stored in a manner to prevent damage and/or contamination?

903. Why are you trying to do it?

904. What happens if your organization fails its Quality

Audit?

905. How does your organization know that its systems for meeting staff extracurricular learning support requirements are appropriately effective and constructive?

906. How is the Strategic Plan (and other plans) reviewed and revised?

907. How does your organization ensure that equipment is appropriately maintained and producing valid results?

908. What review processes are in place for your organizations major activities?

909. How does your organization know that its system for governing staff behaviour is appropriately effective and constructive?

910. How does your organization know that its relationships with other relevant organizations are appropriately effective and constructive?

911. Are all employees including salespersons made aware that they must report all complaints received from any source for inclusion in the complaint handling system?

912. Are goals well supported with strategies, operational plans, manuals and training?

913. How does your organization know that its staff have appropriate access to a fair and effective grievance process?

914. How does your organization know that its public relations and marketing systems are appropriately effective and constructive?

3.6 Team Directory: Privacy Risk

915. Days from the time the issue is identified?

916. Process decisions: are all start-up, turn over and close out requirements of the contract satisfied?

917. Where should the information be distributed?

918. When does information need to be distributed?

919. Contract requirements complied with?

920. Why is the work necessary?

921. Does a Privacy Risk project team directory list all resources assigned to the Privacy Risk project?

922. When will you produce deliverables?

923. Do purchase specifications and configurations match requirements?

924. How do unidentified risks impact the outcome of the Privacy Risk project?

925. Who will be the stakeholders on your next Privacy Risk project?

926. Who should receive information (all stakeholders)?

927. How will you accomplish and manage the objectives?

928. Process decisions: are there any statutory or regulatory issues relevant to the timely execution of work?

929. Decisions: what could be done better to improve the quality of the constructed product?

930. Process decisions: is work progressing on schedule and per contract requirements?

931. Who will write the meeting minutes and distribute?

932. How does the team resolve conflicts and ensure tasks are completed?

933. Process decisions: do job conditions warrant additional actions to collect job information and document on-site activity?

934. Process decisions: which organizational elements and which individuals will be assigned management functions?

3.7 Team Operating Agreement: Privacy Risk

935. Communication protocols: how will the team communicate?

936. Have you established procedures that team members can follow to work effectively together, such as a team operating agreement?

937. How will you resolve conflict efficiently and respectfully?

938. Did you draft the meeting agenda?

939. Do you vary your voice pace, tone and pitch to engage participants and gain involvement?

940. Did you determine the technology methods that best match the messages to be communicated?

941. Methodologies: how will key team processes be implemented, such as training, research, work deliverable production, review and approval processes, knowledge management, and meeting procedures?

942. What resources can be provided for the team in terms of equipment, space, time for training, protected time and space for meetings, and travel allowances?

943. Do team members reside in more than two

countries?

944. Do you solicit member feedback about meetings and what would make them better?

945. Do team members need to frequently communicate as a full group to make timely decisions?

946. Do you brief absent members after they view meeting notes or listen to a recording?

947. What is the anticipated procedure (recruitment, solicitation of volunteers, or assignment) for selecting team members?

948. To whom do you deliver your services?

949. What is a Virtual Team?

950. What is group supervision?

951. Why does your organization want to participate in teaming?

952. Seconds for members to respond?

953. Do you ask participants to close laptops and place mobile devices on silent on the table while the meeting is in progress?

3.8 Team Performance Assessment: Privacy Risk

954. To what degree does the teams purpose constitute a broader, deeper aspiration than just accomplishing short-term goals?

955. What is method variance?

956. How do you encourage members to learn from each other?

957. To what degree can all members engage in open and interactive considerations?

958. To what degree do team members agree with the goals, relative importance, and the ways in which achievement will be measured?

959. What makes opportunities more or less obvious?

960. To what degree are the teams goals and objectives clear, simple, and measurable?

961. To what degree are sub-teams possible or necessary?

962. To what degree does the teams work approach provide opportunity for members to engage in open interaction?

963. When a reviewer complains about method variance, what is the essence of the complaint?

964. How do you manage human resources?

965. How hard do you try to make a good selection?

966. To what degree does the team possess adequate membership to achieve its ends?

967. Which situations call for a more extreme type of adaptiveness in which team members actually re-define roles?

968. How does Privacy Risk project termination impact Privacy Risk project team members?

969. How do you keep key people outside the group informed about its accomplishments?

970. To what degree does the teams approach to its work allow for modification and improvement over time?

971. How hard did you try to make a good selection?

972. To what degree will the approach capitalize on and enhance the skills of all team members in a manner that takes into consideration other demands on members of the team?

3.9 Team Member Performance Assessment: Privacy Risk

973. Should a ratee get a copy of all the raters documents about the employees performance?

974. How is assessment information achieved, stored?

975. Are any governance changes sufficient to impact achievement?

976. Are the draft goals SMART ?

977. Is it clear how goals will be accomplished?

978. Does adaptive training work?

979. How are evaluation results utilized?

980. What is the target group for instruction (e.g., individual and collective or small team instruction)?

981. What instructional strategies were developed/ incorporated (e.g., direct instruction, indirect instruction, experiential learning, independent study, interactive instruction)?

982. How are assessments designed, delivered, and otherwise used to maximize training?

983. To what degree will new and supplemental skills be introduced as the need is recognized?

984. To what degree are the goals realistic?

985. What is used as a basis for instructional decisions?

986. Are the goals SMART ?

987. What evidence supports your decision-making?

988. To what degree do team members understand one anothers roles and skills?

989. To what degree is the team cognizant of small wins to be celebrated along the way?

990. Which training platform formats (i.e., mobile, virtual, videogame-based) were implemented in your effort(s)?

3.10 Issue Log: Privacy Risk

991. What effort will a change need?

992. Why multiple evaluators?

993. Is access to the Issue Log controlled?

994. Persistence; will users learn a work around or will they be bothered every time?

995. Which stakeholders are thought leaders, influences, or early adopters?

996. Are stakeholder roles recognized by your organization?

997. Who reported the issue?

998. What is the stakeholders political influence?

999. Can you think of other people who might have concerns or interests?

1000. What help do you and your team need from the stakeholders?

1001. Which stakeholders can influence others?

1002. Are the Privacy Risk project issues uniquely identified, including to which product they refer?

1003. Who is the stakeholder?

1004. How do you manage communications?

1005. How often do you engage with stakeholders?

1006. What is the status of the issue?

1007. Can an impact cause deviation beyond team, stage or Privacy Risk project tolerances?

4.0 Monitoring and Controlling Process Group: Privacy Risk

1008. Overall, how does the program function to serve the clients?

1009. What is the timeline?

1010. Just how important is your work to the overall success of the Privacy Risk project?

1011. Who needs to be engaged upfront to ensure use of results?

1012. Use: how will they use the information?

1013. Where is the Risk in the Privacy Risk project?

1014. Did you implement the program as designed?

1015. How well did the chosen processes produce the expected results?

1016. Who needs to be involved in the planning?

1017. How many more potential communications channels were introduced by the discovery of the new stakeholders?

1018. Were decisions made in a timely manner?

1019. How can you monitor progress?

1020. How is agile portfolio management done?

1021. How is Agile Privacy Risk project Management done?

1022. Is there sufficient time allotted between the general system design and the detailed system design phases?

1023. Is the schedule for the set products being met?

1024. Is it what was agreed upon?

1025. What factors are contributing to progress or delay in the achievement of products and results?

4.1 Project Performance Report: Privacy Risk

1026. To what degree is the information network consistent with the structure of the formal organization?

1027. Next Steps?

1028. To what degree can team members frequently and easily communicate with one another?

1029. To what degree does the teams work approach provide opportunity for members to engage in results-based evaluation?

1030. To what degree do team members articulate the teams work approach?

1031. To what degree can the team measure progress against specific goals?

1032. To what degree will the team adopt a concrete, clearly understood, and agreed-upon approach that will result in achievement of the teams goals?

1033. To what degree does the formal organization make use of individual resources and meet individual needs?

1034. To what degree are fresh input and perspectives systematically caught and added (for example, through information and analysis, new members, and senior sponsors)?

1035. To what degree does the teams work approach provide opportunity for members to engage in fact-based problem solving?

1036. To what degree do the structures of the formal organization motivate taskrelevant behavior and facilitate task completion?

1037. To what degree does the teams purpose contain themes that are particularly meaningful and memorable?

1038. How is the data used?

1039. To what degree are the demands of the task compatible with and converge with the relationships of the informal organization?

4.2 Variance Analysis: Privacy Risk

1040. Budget versus actual. how does the monthly budget compare to actual experience?

1041. What does an unfavorable overhead volume variance mean?

1042. How do you evaluate the impact of schedule changes, work around, et?

1043. How have the setting and use of standards changed over time?

1044. Is the anticipated (firm and potential) business base Privacy Risk projected in a rational, consistent manner?

1045. How do you verify authorization to proceed with all authorized work?

1046. Are meaningful indicators identified for use in measuring the status of cost and schedule performance?

1047. What is the incurrence of actual indirect costs in excess of budgets, by element of expense?

1048. Does the contractors system identify work accomplishment against the schedule plan?

1049. What is the performance to date and material commitment?

1050. Do you identify potential or actual budget-based and time-based schedule variances?

1051. Are all cwbs elements specified for external reporting?

1052. Are the requirements for all items of overhead established by rational, traceable processes?

1053. What is your organizations rationale for sharing expenses and services between business segments?

1054. Are there changes in the direct base to which overhead costs are allocated?

1055. Favorable or unfavorable variance?

1056. What costs are avoidable if one or more customers are dropped?

1057. How do you identify and isolate causes of favorable and unfavorable cost and schedule variances?

1058. Is there a logical explanation for any variance?

4.3 Earned Value Status: Privacy Risk

1059. Are you hitting your Privacy Risk projects targets?

1060. If earned value management (EVM) is so good in determining the true status of a Privacy Risk project and Privacy Risk project its completion, why is it that hardly any one uses it in information systems related Privacy Risk projects?

1061. How much is it going to cost by the finish?

1062. When is it going to finish?

1063. Earned value can be used in almost any Privacy Risk project situation and in almost any Privacy Risk project environment. it may be used on large Privacy Risk projects, medium sized Privacy Risk projects, tiny Privacy Risk projects (in cut-down form), complex and simple Privacy Risk projects and in any market sector. some people, of course, know all about earned value, they have used it for years - but perhaps not as effectively as they could have?

1064. Where is evidence-based earned value in your organization reported?

1065. Where are your problem areas?

1066. How does this compare with other Privacy Risk projects?

1067. Verification is a process of ensuring that

the developed system satisfies the stakeholders agreements and specifications; Are you building the product right? What do you verify?

1068. Validation is a process of ensuring that the developed system will actually achieve the stakeholders desired outcomes; Are you building the right product? What do you validate?

1069. What is the unit of forecast value?

4.4 Risk Audit: Privacy Risk

1070. Have staff received necessary training?

1071. Does the customer have a solid idea of what is required?

1072. Have you worked with the customer in the past?

1073. The halo effect in business risk audits: can strategic risk assessment bias auditor judgment about accounting details?

1074. Has everyone (staff, volunteers and participants) agreed to a code of behaviour or conduct?

1075. Are regular safety inspections made of buildings, grounds and equipment?

1076. Are some people working on multiple Privacy Risk projects?

1077. Are team members trained in the use of the tools?

1078. Do you have proper induction processes for all new paid staff and volunteers who have a specific role and responsibility?

1079. Do you have written and signed agreements/ contracts in place for each paid staff member?

1080. How effective are your risk controls?

1081. Tradeoff: how much risk can be tolerated and still deliver the products where they need to be?

1082. Are you willing to seek legal advice when required?

1083. Do you promote education and training opportunities?

1084. Does your auditor understand your business?

1085. Are you aware of the industry standards that apply to your operations?

1086. Are all participants informed of safety issues?

1087. Are duties out-of-class?

4.5 Contractor Status Report: Privacy Risk

1088. What are the minimum and optimal bandwidth requirements for the proposed solution?

1089. Are there contractual transfer concerns?

1090. What was the budget or estimated cost for your organizations services?

1091. How is risk transferred?

1092. How does the proposed individual meet each requirement?

1093. How long have you been using the services?

1094. What was the final actual cost?

1095. What was the overall budget or estimated cost?

1096. What process manages the contracts?

1097. Who can list a Privacy Risk project as organization experience, your organization or a previous employee of your organization?

1098. If applicable; describe your standard schedule for new software version releases. Are new software version releases included in the standard maintenance plan?

1099. What was the actual budget or estimated cost for your organizations services?

1100. What is the average response time for answering a support call?

1101. Describe how often regular updates are made to the proposed solution. Are corresponding regular updates included in the standard maintenance plan?

4.6 Formal Acceptance: Privacy Risk

1102. What are the requirements against which to test, Who will execute?

1103. What function(s) does it fill or meet?

1104. Was business value realized?

1105. Do you perform formal acceptance or burn-in tests?

1106. Does it do what client said it would?

1107. General estimate of the costs and times to complete the Privacy Risk project?

1108. Who would use it?

1109. What lessons were learned about your Privacy Risk project management methodology?

1110. What is the Acceptance Management Process?

1111. Did the Privacy Risk project manager and team act in a professional and ethical manner?

1112. Was the Privacy Risk project work done on time, within budget, and according to specification?

1113. Does it do what Privacy Risk project team said it would?

1114. Do you buy pre-configured systems or build

your own configuration?

1115. What features, practices, and processes proved to be strengths or weaknesses?

1116. What was done right?

1117. Who supplies data?

1118. Have all comments been addressed?

1119. Was the Privacy Risk project goal achieved?

1120. What can you do better next time?

1121. Was the sponsor/customer satisfied?

5.0 Closing Process Group: Privacy Risk

1122. Based on your Privacy Risk project communication management plan, what worked well?

1123. Can the lesson learned be replicated?

1124. What can you do better next time, and what specific actions can you take to improve?

1125. Mitigate. what will you do to minimize the impact should a risk event occur?

1126. What was learned?

1127. Were risks identified and mitigated?

1128. When will the Privacy Risk project be done?

1129. Did the Privacy Risk project team have enough people to execute the Privacy Risk project plan?

1130. Were the outcomes different from the already stated planned?

1131. How will you know you did it?

1132. What areas were overlooked on this Privacy Risk project?

1133. Contingency planning. if a risk event occurs,

what will you do?

1134. Is this an updated Privacy Risk project Proposal Document?

1135. What is the risk of failure to your organization?

1136. How dependent is the Privacy Risk project on other Privacy Risk projects or work efforts?

1137. Is there a clear cause and effect between the activity and the lesson learned?

1138. What business situation is being addressed?

1139. Did the Privacy Risk project team have the right skills?

5.1 Procurement Audit: Privacy Risk

1140. Are the purchase order forms designed for efficient and simple completion?

1141. Are proper financing arrangements taken?

1142. Does procurement staff have skills to procure complex or special items (i.e. IT)?

1143. Are individuals with check-signing responsibility prohibited from signing blank checks?

1144. Are risks managed to provide reasonable assurance regarding department procurement objectives?

1145. In case of decisions not to conclude a procurement or award a contract, were tenderers informed in writing and on a timely basis of the already stated decisions and grounds?

1146. Are all initial purchase contracts made by the purchasing organization?

1147. Are required quality and service standards set?

1148. Do the buyers always select or authorize the source of supply on other than contract purchases?

1149. If a purchase order calls for a cost-plus agreement, is the method of determining how final charges will be determined specified?

1150. Is the purchasing department consulted on favorable purchasing opportunities, economic ordering quantities, and revision of purchasing specifications?

1151. In open and restricted procedures, did the contracting authority make sure that there is no substantive change to the bid due to this clearing process?

1152. Does procurement staff have recognized professional procurement qualifications or sufficient training?

1153. Are order quantities, deliveries and payment levels under the contract monitored by an appropriate official?

1154. Are unsuccessful companies informed why tender failed?

1155. Is the efficiency of the procurement process regularly evaluated?

1156. Are regulations and protective measures in place to avoid corruption?

1157. Is there a form specified for bids?

1158. Are checks safeguarded against theft, loss, or misuse?

1159. Could bidders learn all relevant information straight from the tender documents?

5.2 Contract Close-Out: Privacy Risk

1160. Have all contracts been closed?

1161. Have all acceptance criteria been met prior to final payment to contractors?

1162. Why Outsource?

1163. Change in knowledge?

1164. Parties: who is involved?

1165. What is capture management?

1166. Have all contract records been included in the Privacy Risk project archives?

1167. Change in attitude or behavior?

1168. Was the contract complete without requiring numerous changes and revisions?

1169. How does it work?

1170. Have all contracts been completed?

1171. Parties: Authorized?

1172. How is the contracting office notified of the automatic contract close-out?

1173. Has each contract been audited to verify acceptance and delivery?

1174. Change in circumstances?

1175. How/when used ?

1176. Are the signers the authorized officials?

1177. Was the contract sufficiently clear so as not to result in numerous disputes and misunderstandings?

1178. Was the contract type appropriate?

1179. What happens to the recipient of services?

5.3 Project or Phase Close-Out: Privacy Risk

1180. In addition to assessing whether the Privacy Risk project was successful, it is equally critical to analyze why it was or was not fully successful. Are you including this?

1181. Who is responsible for award close-out?

1182. Have business partners been involved extensively, and what data was required for them?

1183. What benefits or impacts does the stakeholder group expect to obtain as a result of the Privacy Risk project?

1184. What was expected from each stakeholder?

1185. When and how were information needs best met?

1186. Is the lesson significant, valid, and applicable?

1187. What were the goals and objectives of the communications strategy for the Privacy Risk project?

1188. What are they?

1189. What were the actual outcomes?

1190. What information is each stakeholder group interested in?

1191. How much influence did the stakeholder have over others?

1192. Planned remaining costs?

1193. What could have been improved?

1194. What stakeholder group needs, expectations, and interests are being met by the Privacy Risk project?

1195. What are the marketing communication needs for each stakeholder?

5.4 Lessons Learned: Privacy Risk

1196. What were the main bottlenecks on the process?

1197. How well did the Privacy Risk project Manager respond to questions or comments related to the Privacy Risk project?

1198. What is the frequency of group communications?

1199. How adequately involved did you feel in Privacy Risk project decisions?

1200. Is there any way in which you think your development process hampered this Privacy Risk project?

1201. What is the desired end-state?

1202. Were quality procedures built into the Privacy Risk project?

1203. What should have been accomplished during predeployment that was not accomplished?

1204. How efficient were Privacy Risk project team meetings conducted?

1205. How smooth do you feel Integration has been?

1206. Why does your organization need a lessons learned (LL) capability?

1207. How effective was each Privacy Risk project Team member in fulfilling his/her role?

1208. How effective were the techniques used to prepare you and your organization for the impact of the changes brought about by the product or service produced by the Privacy Risk project?

1209. Which estimation issues did you personally have and what was the impact?

1210. Was the Privacy Risk project significantly delayed/hampered by outside dependencies (outside to the Privacy Risk project, that is)?

1211. What is the fiscal dependency?

1212. What regulatory constraints impact the case?

1213. How well defined were the acceptance criteria for Privacy Risk project deliverables?

1214. What was the single greatest success and the single greatest shortcoming or challenge from the Privacy Risk projects perspective?

Index

278